APOCALYPSE
RISING

APOCALYPSE
RISING

CHAOS IN THE MIDDLE EAST, THE FALL OF THE
WEST, AND OTHER SIGNS OF THE END TIMES

TIMOTHY
DAILEY, PH.D.

Chosen

a division of Baker Publishing Group
Minneapolis, Minnesota

Published by Chosen Books
11400 Hampshire Avenue South
Bloomington, Minnesota 55438
www.chosenbooks.com

Chosen Books is a division of
Baker Publishing Group, Grand Rapids, Michigan

Printed in the United States of America

Library of Congress Control Number: 2016931353

ISBN 978-0-8007-9798-0

Cover design by Gearbox

16 17 18 19 20 21 22   7 6 5 4 3 2 1

In keeping with biblical principles of creation stewardship, Baker Publishing Group advocates the responsible use of our natural resources. As a member of the Green Press Initiative, our company uses recycled paper when possible. The text paper of this book is composed in part of post-consumer waste.

Contents

Introduction

The End of the World as We Know It

But if we fail, then the whole world . . . including
all that we have known and cared for, will sink into
the abyss of a new Dark Age.
> —Winston Churchill, June 1939

Europe was rent asunder, facing an enemy that appeared unstoppable and bent on conquest. France with her mighty armies had fallen in mere days to the armored columns of the Wehrmacht. The implacable German Führer next set his eyes on Britain and decreed: England must fall!

Attempts to appease Hitler had failed, sweeping Churchill—the one leader with the will to resist the Nazis—into power. The pugnacious Prime Minister stood before Parliament and laid down the gauntlet. "The Battle of Britain has begun," he announced, and "upon this battle depends the survival of Christian civilization." The rest, as they say, is history.

A monstrous evil that eclipses by a quantum leap that of the Third Reich is waiting in the wings to initiate the Final Battle between the forces of good and evil. In the pages that follow we will offer fresh insight into the spreading turmoil in the Middle East and Europe—the United States will not escape—and how it paves the way for the mysterious Gog and Magog of Ezekiel.

Our expansive investigation is a journey back through time spanning more than two millennia, from vast hordes sweeping across Central Asian steppes in search of conquest to present-day geopolitical developments rocking the Middle East, Europe and beyond. We will discover how the lands of Gog and Magog play a role in momentous events in history, from the fall of Rome to the world wars of the twentieth century to the infamous events of 9/11. We will pass through lands scarred by epic battles between East and West—and which are threatened once more by a modern-day invasion from Gog and Magog. We will introduce provocative evidence regarding this question: Is the United States mentioned in the prophetic texts?

Our analysis will reveal a great pincer movement that seeks with one talon to rip apart what remains of Christendom in Europe and the United States while with another talon to rend the Middle East in search of "great spoil." Ultimately we will see that planet Earth is facing catastrophic events of biblical proportion, including threats from space-age doomsday weapons.

Last, but by no means least, we step back to examine a critical weakness that is increasingly found in books on biblical eschatology, leaving more than a few prophecy teachers with egg on their faces. The "atomization of biblical prophecy" leads to detailed charts of end time events that leave little room for the symbolism and vivid imagery that is the hallmark of apocalyptic literature.

Regrettably, this flawed approach can lead to sensationalism and date setting as teachers and writers seek to correlate their intricate prophecy timetables with contemporary events.

The reader is invited to skip ahead and review the afterword, "The Atomization of Biblical Prophecy," which highlights recent claims that biblical prophecies will take place on specific dates—claims that invariably have proven false.

I can still recall, as a young Bible school student, compiling a comprehensive blueprint of end time events, which included a convoluted timeline complete with supporting Scripture texts. It was truly a thing of beauty. It was also an uncritical presentation by a budding and arguably naïve theologian of the views held by the particular denomination in which I had been raised. The years and decades since have (I like to think) brought a greater appreciation for the grandeur and mystery of the biblical prophecies.

The present volume reflects this perspective, which seeks to uncover the historical roots of selected eschatological themes found in Scripture. Together we will explore the fascinating unfolding of the grand eschatological program throughout the ages.

In the Footsteps of Conquerors

The enigmatic Gog and Magog of Ezekiel have been misidentified by a generation of prophecy teachers, many of whom continue to interpret eschatological texts in the light of outdated Cold War politics. The penchant for viewing the Antichrist as a Communist dictator led to the theory that two hundred million Chinese will invade the Holy Land. The Communist Soviet Union came and went after seventy years, while the true lands of Gog and Magog have for millennia harbored enmity toward Christendom—historically Europe—as well as the land of Israel.

A radical new thesis challenges the prevailing ahistorical interpretation of these shadowy foes. Instead of appearing on the world stage suddenly and magically, the ghosts of Gog and Magog have haunted history since the time of Ezekiel, emerging periodically from their remote lair in Asia with "great hordes" of armed horsemen, "all of them brandishing their swords" to rain down terror upon distant lands.

We trace the footsteps of these invaders of old as well as those kingdoms and empires that sought—unsuccessfully—to defeat them, foreshadowing a war of cosmic proportions at the climax of human history. We will see that the lands of Gog and Magog have historically been an indomitable and mysterious region that will one day instigate the battle at the end of the world.

The Iron Gates of Alexander

Our story begins with the legendary iron gates constructed to hold back the barbaric raiders from Gog and Magog, where we cross paths with perhaps the greatest conqueror the world has ever known. Alexander the Great set out to vanquish Persia, the ancient enemy of Greece, and from there to continue eastward until he had subjugated India. Undefeated on the battlefield, Alexander's advance was nonetheless checked as he sought to conquer barbarians from the north. According to lore that stirred imaginations in Europe for a thousand years, he constructed immense iron gates to bar their way to the civilized world.

A Race Savage Beyond All Parallel

The malignant force from beyond Alexander's gates waited, biding its time. It reemerged through nomadic invaders known as the Huns. Led by Attila, these primitive warriors from the Asian steppes swept largely unopposed into Europe. They forced out other peoples, setting into motion a savage chain reaction that culminated in the sack of Rome. After a period of relative calm, the Huns initiated a determined attack on the entire Roman Empire, driven in part thanks to a scheming princess.

A Medieval Blitzkrieg

Centuries later Europe was once again the focus of a great invasion. The Mongol hordes of Genghis Khan wrought unprecedented devastation as they marched westward to Poland, Hungary and the Balkans—and south into the Middle East. The trademarks of what would become the largest contiguous empire in history included the slaughter of entire cities and the deliberate use of the bubonic plague to decimate their enemies. These nomadic predecessors of the Ottoman Turks also stormed out of central Asia—the land of Gog and Magog.

The Gates of Vienna

It is in Vienna, that sentinel on the Danube and gateway to the West, that we encounter yet another historic conqueror from Gog and Magog: Suleiman the Magnificent, greatest Sultan of the Ottoman Empire. Not once but twice, the fate of Christendom hung in the balance before the walls of Vienna as the beleaguered garrison held off the assault of the Ottoman armies, facing slaughter or enslavement and praying for a miracle. Just as it appeared all hope was lost, Polish king John III Sobieski swept down from the heights to save the day.

The Disintegrating Middle East

Moving into the present day, we examine the chaos descending upon the lands of the Bible. At root is a fierce Arabian faith that has sought through the centuries to subjugate Jews and Christians through the command to engage in *jihad* (holy war) against the "infidel." The Middle East is awash with Islamic factions, each more radical than the last, all determined to restore the caliphate—a worldwide Islamic state built upon the blood of Christian martyrs who are being called upon to make the ultimate sacrifice at the astounding rate of one every five minutes.

Tangled Alliances

In the midst of profound upheaval in Muslim lands of the Middle East and North Africa, a new terrorist organization has burst upon the scene, driven by a brutal fanaticism and subjecting those under its control to unparalleled levels of savagery. Gruesome decapitations have become commonplace, as if in fulfillment of the book of Revelation: "I saw the souls of those who had been beheaded for the testimony of Jesus and for the word of God" (Revelation 20:4 ESV).

Jihad by Other Means

More than three centuries after the Turkish assault upon the gates of Vienna, another great invasion from the East would threaten the Christian civilization of Europe in our day. This time the attack would come not by armies brandishing swords but by masses of refugees fleeing the ravages of armed conflict. And like the multitudes driven across the Danube by the Huns of old, these migrants—some of whom refuse to assimilate but seek to promulgate an alien ideology—are irrevocably changing the face of Europe. Even more disconcerting, we are now seeing how agents secreted among the legitimate asylum seekers are working to destabilize the continent through senseless acts of violence.

Israel's Newfound Energy Wealth

Sowing chaos in Europe is but one tactic of the nefarious Beast: The book of Ezekiel reveals that in the last days Gog and Magog will be pulled by "hooks in [their] jaws" (38:4) to invade the Middle East. Their intention is to "plunder and loot" (38:12). The identification of the source of this great wealth has eluded commentators—until now. Astonishingly, the Jewish state has gone from energy dependence to being potentially a supplier of valuable energy sources that promise to be hotly contested by Israel's enemies. A *casus belli*?

Ships of Tarshish

In the midst of Ezekiel's prophecy about a cataclysmic invasion of Israel, we read that "the merchants of Tarshish and all her villages" (i.e., colonies) rise up to confront Gog and Magog. Tarshish was located on the southwestern coast of Spain—the very port of embarkation for Christopher Columbus as he set sail for the New World. The historical evidence extending the far-flung colonies of Tarshish to the Americas provides a link between the United States and biblical prophecy.

Have You Come to Take Great Plunder?

The connection between America and "Tarshish and her colonies" prompts a question that has eluded biblical commentators: What could be the possible role of the United

States in the end times? Two interpretations of the challenge "Have you come to take great plunder?" have polar opposite consequences for the unfolding of the biblical prophecies. The first is that the United States, weakened by internal division, is both unwilling and unable to intercede for Israel. The second is that Western Christendom—led by a resurgent America—will overcome the threat to its historic religion and culture, enabling it to stand with Israel against the Antichrist in the final battle.

The ambiguity—we suggest—is entirely by design, and intended to present 21st-century America with an opportunity to join the forces of good in the end time battle. But only if the Sleeping Giant is awakened in time.

The Doomsday Scenario

Next we turn our attention to a perplexing passage in the book of Revelation that speaks of Mystery Babylon being destroyed "in an hour." Unimaginable until the present day, a doomsday scenario now exists whereby life as we know it could come to a screeching halt for tens of millions. The possibility is nearing for a low-yield nuclear-tipped ballistic missile to trigger a massive electromagnetic pulse (EMP) that in a millisecond could destroy a nation's electrical grid along with virtually all electronic devices and components for an indefinite period of time. The enemies of the United States and Israel are already experimenting with EMP technology.

Solar Storm

We examine even greater threats: Earth could one day come under attack from X rays, charged particles and magnetized plasma ejected from explosions on the surface of the sun. Such a gigantic "solar storm" could wipe out the technology and electric power grids of the entire planet. The largest of these events—X-class flares—could spew out as much energy as a billion hydrogen bombs.

But Before All These Things

Indeed, Jesus warned His disciples that "fearful events" and "great signs from heaven" would cause unprecedented devastation at the end of days. Jesus stipulated, however, that before all these things came to pass, His followers would endure great suffering. Jesus' description of those days indicates that the legal system will be used to oppress Christians, who will be arrested, tried by the authorities and thrown into "prison." For the first time since the days of the early Church, legal charges, onerous fines and even jail time are being levied against believers in the so-called Christian West for the "offense" of seeking to remain true to their faith. Should this sinister trend continue, it could remove the one great impediment to identifying the United States as Mystery Babylon.

The Name that Overcomes

This litany of horrors is not the stuff of fevered imagination: Each can arguably be deduced from the eschatological texts. Yet we must remember the command given to the prophet Daniel, "Seal the words of the scroll until the time of the end" (12:4) and confess that "for now we see through a glass, darkly" (1 Corinthians 13:12 KJV). The cryptic nature of the apocalyptic genre leaves open the possibility of variant outcomes, and we have a great hope that the Light will shine through the darkness. We shall explore all this and more. Let the journey begin!

PART 1

KINGDOMS
OF GOG
AND MAGOG

1

Out of the Far North

Chapters 38 and 39 of Ezekiel describe a great conflict at the end of the age: the battle "against Gog, of the land of Magog." This enigmatic and difficult passage has been the subject of endless discussion and speculation among Bible scholars as to the identification of the mysterious participants.

One view holds that the text is referring to a Russian-led invasion of the Middle East. This interpretation arose during the Cold War when the atheistic Soviet Union—of which Russia was the principal republic—was deeply involved in the Middle East. It made perfect sense in a day when Russia was supplying Israel's hostile Arab neighbors with military equipment that was used to attack the Jewish state. One prominent advocate of this view, John F. Walvoord, stated assuredly that Ezekiel 38 and 39 "could only refer to what we know today as Russia."[1]

Then came the fall of the Soviet Union, and prophecy teachers were left without their Evil Empire. A surprising number plowed along undeterred, continuing to insist that Russia is destined to invade Israel at the end of days. A growing number of scholars, however, realize that the Russian invasion theory rests upon scanty foundations.

The setting of Ezekiel's prophecy is an invasion of Israel by Gog and Magog at a time when the land has been restored after a long period of desolation:

> After many days you will be called to arms. In future years you will invade a land that has recovered from war, whose people were gathered from many nations to the mountains of Israel, which had long been desolate. They had been brought out from the nations, and now all of them live in safety.
>
> Ezekiel 38:8

The characterization of Israel as a land "which had long been desolate" is an apt description of the historical period between the second century and the late nineteenth century. After the Second Jewish Revolt (AD 132–136) was crushed, Jews were banned from Judea, which was renamed *Palaestina* by the victorious Romans. Although Jews were later allowed to return, by the Middle Ages the land had been impoverished by conflict and the population severely reduced.

When author Mark Twain visited the Holy Land in 1867, he described a desolate Galilee: "There is not a solitary village throughout its whole extent—not for thirty miles in either direction. There are two or three small clusters of Bedouin [nomadic Arabian] tents, but not a single permanent habitation. One may ride ten miles, hereabouts, and not see ten human beings."[2]

Ezekiel prophesied that "after many days . . . in future years" (38:8) a restored land of Israel will be invaded by the armies of Gog and Magog. Mark Twain would be astonished to see Israeli Galilee today, a prosperous land teeming with bountiful agriculture and bustling cities and towns.

In like manner the visitor to modern Jerusalem with a population approaching one million would scarcely recognize Twain's description of a neglected city of some fourteen thousand impoverished residents:

> Rags, wretchedness, poverty and dirt, those signs and symbols that indicate the presence of Moslem rule more surely than the crescent-flag itself, abound. Lepers, cripples, the blind, and the idiotic, assail you on every hand, and they know but one word of but one language apparently—the eternal "bucksheesh." To see the numbers of maimed, malformed and diseased humanity that throng the holy places and obstruct the gates, one might suppose that the ancient days had come again, and that the angel of the Lord was expected to descend at any moment to stir the waters of Bethesda. Jerusalem is mournful, and dreary, and lifeless.[3]

We are also told that the invasion will occur at a time when the regathered Jews "live in safety" (Ezekiel 38:8). One interpretation is that the inhabitants have been lulled by a false sense of safety. The text can also refer to a high state of security in the face of threats.[4] This would certainly describe the level of military readiness in Israel against domestic terrorist threats and hostile neighboring states. The invasion of Gog and Magog, however, will originate from distant lands.

North by Northeast

Ezekiel 38 specifies the direction of the attack: "You will come from your place in the far north, you and many nations with you, all of them riding on horses, a great horde, a mighty army" (Ezekiel 38:15). The proponents of the Russia-led invasion theory point to this verse, and indeed a line drawn straight north from Israel could scarcely avoid bisecting the largest country on the globe.

It is by no means certain that this text refers to Russia, as many references to the north in the Bible actually refer to Eastern lands. The book of Jeremiah warns repeatedly of a coming invasion by the Babylonians, which took place in 586 BC: "Raise the signal to go to Zion! Flee for safety without delay! For I am bringing disaster *from the north*, even terrible destruction" (Jeremiah 4:6, emphasis added). A quick check of maps of the Middle East in biblical times shows that Babylon was not north of Israel but rather was directly east.

Similarly, Jeremiah foretells the defeat of Pharaoh Necho II at Carchemish, which occurred in 605 BC: "Daughter Egypt will be put to shame, given into the hands of the people *of the north*" (Jeremiah 46:24, emphasis added). The Egyptian army was defeated by the neo-Babylonian army led by Nebuchadnezzar. Once again the Babylonians are depicted as coming from the north. In another passage Assyria is also described as located in "the north" even though its capital, Nineveh, lies to the east of Israel (see Zephaniah 2:13).

The explanation as to why the Bible speaks of people from Eastern lands coming from the north lies in the geography of the region. The biblical world has been called "the Fertile Crescent," a boomerang-shaped swath of arable land that follows the Tigris and Euphrates Rivers up to northern Syria before continuing west and curving back down toward the Holy Land. In the middle lies the inhospitable Syrian-Arabian desert, which was virtually impassable except for camel-riding Bedouin. Travelers in olden times circumvented the desert, following instead the well-watered Fertile Crescent, where most of the trading cities of the region were located. Abraham followed this route, sojourning at Haran in northern Syria along the way.

The armies of Assyria and Babylon also marched along this route; hence the biblical references to Israel being invaded from the north. The texts are indicating the direction of the invasion, not the place of the invader's origin.

As noted, the wording of texts in Ezekiel that refer to "the far north" has led to speculation that Russia is in view; however, a similar wording is used in Jeremiah 6:22, which speaks of the Babylonian invasion as coming from "the ends of the earth." Even more telling, Ezekiel also refers to Beth Togarmah as coming "from the far north" (38:6). As for the geographical region of Togarmah, Mark Hitchcock states the general consensus: "Togarmah was both the name of a district and a city in the border of Tubal in eastern Cappadocia."[5]

Cappadocia was located in what is now Turkey, a region that was in olden times known as Asia Minor. Thus, to the biblical writer "far north" referred to modern Turkey. While the Russian-led invasion theory seemed to fit the geopolitics of the Cold War, it lacks exegetical support—superficial linguistic similarities between Rosh/Russia, Meshech/Moscow notwithstanding. What, then, can be known about the mysterious invaders of the land of Israel in the end times?

Gog and Magog

The identity of Gog in Ezekiel 38 and 39 remains uncertain.[6] A king, Gugu, who is identified with Gyges, king of Lydia, is mentioned in the Assyrian texts. Lydia was a kingdom in eastern Asia Minor, and the reign of Gyges (c. 660 BC) is also roughly contemporary with the book of Ezekiel, suggesting that the prophet was referring to the Lydian king.

The name *Magog* is not mentioned in the Assyrian literature, our primary source for the eighth and seventh centuries BC. Writing in the first century AD, Jewish historian Josephus provides our initial clue: "Magog founded the Magogians, thus named after him, but who by the Greeks are called Scythians."[7]

The proponents of the theory identifying Gog and Magog with Russia note, correctly, that the Scythians were horse-riding nomads who originated from the steppes of southern Russia. By the time of Ezekiel in the seventh century BC, however, they had crossed the Caucasus, which straddles the Black and Caspian Seas. From there they spread into Asia Minor—modern Turkey—and projected their power to the Middle East and the Iranian Plateau, where they participated in the sack of Nineveh and the destruction of the Assyrian Empire.

In 329 BC, the Scythians were defeated by Alexander the Great and his Macedonian army at the Battle of Jaxartes. This is the Scythia that Josephus identifies as Gog and Magog: a region roughly contiguous with Turkey, extending eastward to the Central Asian Republics.

Rosh, Meshech and Tubal

Ezekiel mentions as co-conspirators of Gog and Magog the evil triumvirate of Rosh, Meshech and Tubal. The Russian-led invasion theory identifies these as Russia, Moscow and Tobolsk based upon the resemblance of the names. Proponents also quote a nineteenth-century work: Gesenius' *Hebrew and English Lexicon*:

> Gesenius, whose Hebrew Lexicon has never been superseded, says that "Gog" is "undoubtedly the Russians." He declared that "Rosh" was a designation for the tribes then north of the Taurus mountains, . . . and in this name of tribe we have the first trace in history of the "Russ" or Russian nation. Gesenius also identified "Meshech" as Moscow, the capital of modern Russia in Europe. "Tubal" he identified as Tobolsk, the earliest province of Asiatic Russia to be colonized.[8]

The early editions of Gesenius, however, have been superseded by later revisions of his own work as well as standard texts

24

such as the *Theological Dictionary of the Old Testament*, none of which includes his oft-quoted but misinformed views about Rosh, Meshech and Tubal. Eminent Assyriologist D. J. Wiseman speaks for many in rejecting the Russian identification: "Gesenius suggested Russia, but this name is not attested in the area, and a very distant people named this early is unlikely in the context."[9]

Fortunately, we are not dependent upon superficial and misleading phonetic similarity: There is ample historical evidence identifying "Rosh" with the Assyrian place name "Rashu" located in a region stretching across what is now northern Iran and Azerbaijan. As such, their only connection with Russia was during the nineteenth century under Alexander I and for seventy years in the twentieth century when Azerbaijan was part of the Soviet Union.

Any connection between Tubal and the Russian city of Tobolsk must be regarded as specious. Tobolsk was founded in AD 1587, when Siberia was colonized by the Russian empire, and is thus a latecomer on the stage of human history. On firmer footing is the view expressed by T. C. Mitchell that Meshech and Tubal are correctly associated with "the people referred to as Tabal and Musku in the Assyrian inscriptions and Tibareroi and Moschoi in Herodotus, in both of which sources these names are closely associated."[10]

As to their geographic location, the Assyrian cuneiform texts clearly locate Tabal and Musku in central and eastern Anatolia (the Asian landmass of modern Turkey).

One may thus wholeheartedly concur with Joseph Blenkinsopp, who, noting the persistence of the unfounded Russia-led Gog and Magog invasion theory, states, "So it is still necessary to repeat that *ro'sh meshech* has nothing to do, etymologically or otherwise, with Russia and Moscow."[11]

We are starting to discern a pattern: The outlines of a geographic region that corresponds to the biblical references to Gog and Magog are beginning to emerge. This area includes Anatolia and northern Iran and stretches eastward to encompass other Turkic peoples of Central Asia. Let us now examine what can be said about the other four participants in the great end time battle of Gog and Magog.

The Allies of Gog

Ezekiel mentions the confederates of Gog and Magog: "Persia, Cush and Put will be with them, all with shields and helmets, also Gomer with all its troops, and Beth Togarmah from the far north with all its troops—the many nations with you" (Ezekiel 38:5–6). There is general consensus regarding the first three of the remaining allies of Gog and Magog. *Persia* was the name of Iran until 1959, when the government of Shah Mohammad Reza Pahlavi changed it to Iran. *Cush* was another name for the Nubian kingdom of Ethiopia and is so identified in numerous translations. *Put* was one of the sons of Ham (see Genesis 10:6) who according to Josephus founded Libya.[12]

As for the final ally, *Gomer*, proponents of a Russian-led invasion are at pains to connect it to the Soviet Union. Hal Lindsey popularized the view that it refers to East Germany: "The conclusion is that Gomer and its hordes are part of the vast area of modern Eastern Europe which is totally behind the Iron Curtain. This includes East Germany and the Slovak countries."[13] As part of the now defunct Soviet-allied Warsaw Pact, this identification seemed to fit the picture of a Russian-led invasion of the Middle East.

Lindsey cites the aforementioned discredited view of Gesenius, who stands alone among linguists with his novel identifications of Gog and its allies. One searches critical and exegetical commentaries in vain for support of the view that Gomer is East Germany. The scholarly consensus is summarized by Walther Eichrodt:

[The people of Gomer are] referred to by the Assyrians as Gimir-rai, and by the Greeks as Cimmerians. They emerge in the eighth century as conquerors of Urartu (Armenia) in Asia Minor and then as invaders of the territory of the Phrygians and Lydians.[14]

Once again we see a connection to Anatolia: The Cimmerians occupied the southern shores of the Black Sea in what is now eastern Turkey. As we have already seen, Beth Togarmah occupied central Asia Minor—the same geographic region where Meshech, Tubal and Gomer are located.

Thus the available evidence suggests that the primary participants in the future invasion of Israel hail from the region encompassed by Turkey, northern Iran and the southernmost Central Asian Republics. Some expand this confederacy to include the neighboring Xinjiang Uyghur Autonomous Region of China based upon its ethnic and religious ties with Turkey and Central Asia. Support also comes from confederates in the general area of Libya and Ethiopia in North Africa.

We shall see presently how these archenemies of all that is good will not appear suddenly, as it were, out of thin air. Rather, they have been with us all along. But first we will examine another passage in Revelation that is often misinterpreted by commentators who envision yet another battle to complicate events at the end of time—this one involving a fantastical army of two hundred million soldiers advancing from the East.

2

Invasion from the East

> The sixth angel poured out his bowl on the great
> river Euphrates, and its water was dried up to pre-
> pare the way for the kings from the East.
>
> Revelation 16:12

This cryptic verse in the book of Revelation has been the source of unending speculation by prophecy teachers. Hal Lindsey is a proponent of one view regarding the identification of the "kings from the East" that was popular during the Cold War era:

> We believe that China is the beginning of the formation of this great power called "the kings of the east" by the apostle John. . . . In fact, a recent television documentary on Red China . . . quoted the boast of the Chinese themselves that they could field a "people's army" of 200 million militiamen. In their boast they named the same number as the biblical prediction. Coincidence?[1]

This theory seemed to make sense in a day when Mao Tse-tung ruled over a heavily militarized 25 percent of the world's population, especially when paired with another verse from Revelation:

> And the four angels who had been kept ready for this very hour and day and month and year were released to kill a third of mankind. The number of the mounted troops was twice ten thousand times ten thousand. I heard their number.
>
> Revelation 9:15–16

Those who anticipate a Chinese invasion of the Middle East connect these verses with the "kings from the East" verse, arguing that these passages can only be referring to the world's most populous nation. There is, however, no direct relation between the two passages. In addition to the fact that Revelation 9:15–16 mentions no kings, it is not at all clear that human soldiers are indicated. The text continues on to describe fearsome creatures:

> The horses and riders I saw in my vision looked like this: Their breastplates were fiery red, dark blue, and yellow as sulfur. The heads of the horses resembled the heads of lions, and out of their mouths came fire, smoke and sulfur. A third of mankind was killed by the three plagues of fire, smoke and sulfur that came out of their mouths. The power of the horses was in their mouths and in their tails; for their tails were like snakes, having heads with which they inflict injury.
>
> Revelation 9:17–19

This depiction of "horses and riders" is most likely intended to be anthropomorphic (attributing human characteristics to nonhuman creatures). Horses do not expel "fire, smoke and sulfur" from their mouths, nor do they sport "tails . . . like snakes." Rather, these mounted soldiers are likely fearsome demonic beings that defy description. As typically occurs in

30

the eschatological texts, the biblical writer must use limited human language to portray unearthly visions.

Setting aside for a moment the fact that the People's Liberation Army is currently 1.6 million strong, let's examine the sheer logistics of transporting two hundred million Chinese soldiers with their weaponry to the Middle East. During the Gulf War (1990–1991), it took the United States six months to move half a million troops and their equipment to the war zone. It was the greatest air- and sealift in human history, but it pales in comparison to the task of moving many millions of soldiers from the East.

Assuming that the Chinese army could be moved at the same rate, it would take a full *two centuries* to move a two-hundred-million-man army to the Middle East. Such an army would require some ten million vehicles to move the soldiers and their weapons, equipment and supplies. If we calculate an average of forty yards of road space between vehicles, such a convoy would stretch for 227,000 miles, or *almost ten times around the circumference of the earth*. Finally, once they arrived they would face the difficulty of squeezing such an enormous army into the tiny country of Israel, let alone finding space to maneuver.

Let us state the obvious: The notion of a two-hundred-million-man Chinese army invading Israel, a major tenet of legions of prophecy books, is wholly without foundation and frankly ridiculous. It is also an indictment of the "herd mentality" of prophecy teachers and writers who are unwilling to challenge popular but unfounded theories.

Islam in the Middle Kingdom

We are still left to identify the "kings from the East." We have seen that Gog and Magog are neither historically nor geographically associated with Russia. Likewise, there is no biblical justification for the theory that "kings from the East" refers to a Chinese invasion of Israel. Neither Russia nor China has ever indicated a desire to invade the Jewish state; nor can it be shown that these two world powers possess a cultural or ideological rationale for such an invasion.

The region stretching from Anatolia eastward across northern Iran and the southernmost Central Asian Republics, on the other hand, fits the requirements of the biblical texts regarding Gog and Magog and the "kings from the East." These peoples and lands share one characteristic: They are Turkic in origin. The Turks have been associated with the aforementioned Scythians—whom the ancients identified with Gog and Magog.

The adjoining Xinjiang Uyghur Autonomous Region of China would be a natural fit for the confederacy. The Uyghur inhabitants of Xinjiang are ethnically related to Turkey, and historically the area was known as Chinese Turkestan until it was formally incorporated into the People's Republic of China in 1949. About half of Xinjiang is Muslim, compared to only 2 percent of the main body of China. Radical Muslim groups such as the East Turkestan Islamic Movement have in recent years fomented violent protests in which hundreds of Uyghurs have died.

The Chinese government has voiced concern that foreign jihadists are behind the unrest, and the BBC reports that the Islamic State of Iraq and Syria (ISIS) leader Abu Bakr al-Baghdadi has publicly called on all Chinese Muslims to pledge allegiance to him: "An English-language magazine released by al-Qaeda described Xinjiang as an occupied Muslim land to be recovered into the Caliphate."[2]

In an attempt to stem radicalism in Xinjiang, the Chinese government has taken steps to suppress Muslim practices. In response to a growing number of deadly bombings, Beijing announced "a year-long campaign against terrorism" in 2014. In a move that only inflamed passions, Muslim civil servants,

teachers and students were banned from fasting during Ramadan, and Muslim shops and restaurants were ordered to sell
cigarettes and alcohol or be shut down. The public wearing
of burkas—a one-piece veil that covers a woman's face and
body—was outlawed. Steep fines were levied on anyone dis-
seminating Islamist ideology through the Internet.

These repressive measures, which defied fundamental Muslim
belief and practice, only exasperated tensions and provided fod-
der for the radicals in Xinjiang who are calling for secession in
favor of joining a Muslim caliphate. But, as always, China takes
the long view, and knows that Islam poses a mortal threat to the
interests of the Middle Kingdom—both at home and abroad.

A Sino-Soviet Axis?

We can determine that both the identification of Russia as Gog
and the proposition that China will launch an attack with a
two-hundred-million-man army lack exegetical support. Yet
this does not exclude these two great nations from taking part
in end time events. Evidence indicates that, far from leading an
invasion against Israel, both China and Russia will be at odds
with Gog and Magog.

In the Middle East, China is determined to safeguard the
source of fully half of its oil imports, the lifeblood of its economy. China, as with other observers, recognizes that ISIS poses
the greatest threat to peace and security. In late 2015, in an
unprecedented move, Chinese warships—including an aircraft
carrier—passed through the Suez Canal headed for the eastern
Mediterranean. In what could be yet another ominous escala-
tion, China was reported to be considering sending military
advisors to Syria.[3]

Russia, for her part, has reasserted herself in the Middle East
in force after transforming a neglected airfield in Latakia, Syria,

into a strategic center for military operations against ISIS. The airstrip is capable of accepting Antonov transport aircraft and has bays for more than fifty bombers, ground-support fighters and helicopter gunships. The base has also become home to air-defense systems and armored-personnel carriers, and it has housing for thousands of soldiers and support personnel.

A History of Enmity

The theory that Russia as Gog will join Turkey in an attack on Israel runs counter to both history and the contemporary geopolitics of the Middle East. In one of the longest conflicts in Europe, between the sixteenth and the twentieth centuries, the Turkish Ottoman Empire and Russia fought no fewer than twelve major wars. Behind the various political reasons for the mutual hostilities lay the fundamental religious conflict between the Muslim caliphate and Orthodox Christian Russia.

For a decade, beginning in the 1990s, Russia fought two devastating Chechen wars in the Caucasus against Muslim separatists. Grozny, the capital of Chechnya in southwest Russia, was largely destroyed, with one hundred thousand people killed. Chechnya lies in the midst of a swath of predominantly Muslim countries extending from Turkey to Xinjiang—the very lands of Gog and Magog. The Islamist movement sweeping the Caucasus has already impacted the United States, as the Tsarnaev brothers—the 2013 "Boston Bombers"—had roots in next-door Dagestan.

The Syrian conflict has exposed growing strains between Turkey and Russia. After being elected to Russia's presidency in 2012 for a third term, Vladimir Putin announced that he intended to provide military assistance to Syria's two million Kurds. While the United States views the Kurds as allies, Turkey views them as supporting Kurdish separatist groups within her borders. Incursions of Russian aircraft into Turkish airspace have also provoked strong warnings from Ankara. In November 2015 tensions between the two countries came to a head when Turkish F-16 warplanes shot down a Russian Su-24 jet that it claimed had violated its airspace, killing one of the pilots.

The "Russian invasion of Israel" theory remains stuck in the Cold War era, when the atheistic Soviet Union fomented Communist revolution around the globe and supported the Arabs in order to increase its influence—and promote socialism—in the Middle East. Since the fall of the Soviet Union in 1991, there has been a resurgence of Christianity in Russia and a change of national priorities.

Russia has developed a positive relationship with the very target of Gog and Magog. Moscow and Jerusalem are enjoying close cooperation within a number of mutual interests and have exchanged high-level military delegations. Trade between the two countries, including armaments, continues to increase. During her military buildup in Syria, Russia reached a bilateral understanding with Israel, coordinating military operations in order to safeguard the respective interests of both countries.

It is wholly incongruous to claim that Russia and China, nations with long histories of hostility against the lands of Gog and Magog, nations that are battling Muslim extremism—the predominate religion of those selfsame lands—and nations that enjoy good relations with Israel are in fact Gog and Magog. By contrast, Turkey, Iran and their Muslim confederates have long histories of hostility against the Jewish people and the land of Israel.

Thus we can safely conclude that the battle of Gog and Magog and the invasion of the "kings from the East" involve the same Turkish people along with their confederates and are in all likelihood the same eschatological event.

It is no coincidence that Gog and Magog are associated with a region that has engendered some of the most brutal warfare known to humankind. We will now look at the great invasions associated with this region—led by some of the most renowned conquerors of human history—and reveal fascinating clues about the malevolent forces behind these expansionist movements.

3

The Gates of Alexander

There is a story told about Alexander the Great, which like much of his life is shrouded in legend but may in fact be based upon a kernel of historical truth. As the armies of the young Macedonian conqueror smashed the Persian defenses on the plain of Gaugamela, the road to the East and uncharted lands beyond lay open. Emboldened by prophecies of world conquest uttered at Gordium in Asia Minor and by the High Priest in Jerusalem—and confirmed at the Temple of Amun in the Egyptian desert—Alexander set his face toward the farthest extent of the known world: India.

Alexander's dream of subjugating the entire empire of the Indus would be cut short on windswept Asian steppes when he ventured northward into uncharted regions beyond what the Greeks considered the civilized world. Here, for the first time, the advance of his army was checked. He clashed with an alien nomadic people who proved so intractable that after his initial victory at Jaxartes he was forced to cut his losses and turn back, resuming his conquest of India.

But by then Alexander's army, depleted by three years of warfare in the north, whose stony ground held the most fallen Hellenic soldiers of any of his campaigns, lost its taste for conquest. They refused to continue, pleading that they "longed to again see their parents, their wives and children, their homeland." Neither bribes nor threats—nor the specter of a sullen Alexander retreating to his tent for days—would change the minds of his weary soldiers.

As he turned his face away from the fabled glories of India, forever lost to him, Alexander had one last score to settle. These nomadic people who displayed such skill as warriors on the battlefield left an indelible impression upon him. Such was his alarm at the threat the northern barbarians posed to Western lands that, the sources of old tell us, he constructed a great barrier to prevent the Scythians from invading and wreaking havoc on the civilized world.[1]

These gates were said to have been situated in the southern reaches of the Caucasus in Georgia, whose kings were described in early medieval sources as the guardians of the Gates of Alexander. Similarly, on the far side of Asia, the monumental Great Wall of China was first constructed by the Han Dynasty to keep out the selfsame marauding nomads from central Asia—the very invaders identified as Gog and Magog.

Central Asia is a land steeped in arcane history, including the legend of Prestor John, who according to Marco Polo established a hidden Christian kingdom that was lost amidst the Muslims and pagans in the Orient. The medievals were also fascinated by another mysterious kingdom: that of the Khazars, said to be descendants of Gog and Magog. In a bizarre twist, according to some sources the leaders of the Khazars converted to Judaism. Muslim eschatology speaks of a warrior king called

Dhul-Qarnayn, who erected a wall of iron to imprison Gog and Magog in central Asia until the end of days, when they will escape to "do great mischief upon the earth."

Where Satan Has His Throne

For the Greeks, the Caucasus fringed the known world. It was there that Aeschylus' Prometheus was exiled, bound by Zeus to an inaccessible rock as eternal punishment for bestowing the gift of fire upon men. Seven centuries before Josephus' time, Hesiod, father of Greek didactic poetry and literature, associated Magog with the Scythians, a fiercely nomadic people who at that time occupied wide swaths of the Asian steppes north of the Caucasus.

Greek historian Herodotus also identified these obscure warriors, who defied the likes of Alexander, as Scythians. Throughout history, invaders with familiar names—Huns, Mongols and Turks—would sally forth from this vast, unfathomable land that others—Persians, Romans and Greeks—alternately sought to subjugate.

It was a sweeping clash of civilizations, East versus West, that ranged across two millennia. The center of geopolitical power was situated at the juncture of Europe and the great Iranian civilizations, with India beyond. To the south lay Syria, Arabia and Egypt. Overshadowing all in the impenetrable north, the Scythians defied every attempt to subdue them.

But the Scythians are part of an even deeper enigma for, as noted, the early sources connect them to the mysterious Gog and Magog of the biblical apocalypse who lead a final rebellion against God. We find tantalizing archaeological clues from this arcane region. The ancient capital city of Pergamon, situated in eastern Anatolia, is identified in Revelation as the very place "where Satan has his throne" (2:13).

An imposing forty-foot-high altar of Zeus, uncovered by archaeologists, contains further unsettling clues as to the presence of malignant powers. Ares, the Greek god of war—so brutal that his own mythological parents, Zeus and Hera, hated him—is cryptically depicted here. Students of biblical prophecy ask, Will a modern Ares one day unleash a cataclysmic war upon the globe? In another connection with mystical forces of evil, the city was also a major center of devotion to Asclepius, called "the Greek serpent god of healing and the underworld."[2]

In the Roman city of Hierapolis—also in eastern Turkey—archaeologists recently uncovered yet another enigmatic connection to biblical prophecy. The site, known as Pluto's Gate, was celebrated in Greco-Roman mythology and tradition as the portal to the underworld, bringing to mind this promise of Jesus: "On this rock I will build my church, and the gates of Hades will not overcome it" (Matthew 16:18).

Archaeologists have uncovered a Greek temple at the site built around a cave leading deep underground.[3] To this day noxious vapors issue from the cave, which kill birds that fly too close to the aperture. A large statue uncovered at the site depicts Hades, Greek god of the underworld.

There are indications that Jesus might have been referring to Hierapolis when He mentioned the gateway to Hades. As the site was a major pilgrimage destination in the Greco-Roman world, it was likely known to the disciples of Jesus. According to tradition, the apostle Philip journeyed to Hierapolis to preach and suffered martyrdom there.

At its height, Hierapolis boasted splendid temples, a theater and sacred hot springs, and continued to be active for centuries. But such was the wariness on the part of the Christianized Roman Empire concerning this gateway to the underworld that the site was razed in the sixth century AD.

Centuries would pass and kingdoms would come and go. In due time the land of Gog and Magog would wake from its slumber, issuing forth a series of great conquerors and empires. Their names are familiar, but we might be unaware of the intriguing connection they shared. Christendom and its riches were the ultimate prize—and considered fair game for those who spurned any way of life but their own.

In our day we are seeing an unprecedented invasion of the continent of Europe by those who consider themselves to be fulfilling the command of Allah to subjugate the unbeliever—and who are pursuing jihad by other means. But first we turn our attention to the forerunners of Gog and Magog who struck terror in the hearts of all those who stood in their path.

Hell Hath No Fury

If history is any guide, rejecting the marriage proposal of a world conqueror on the march is a faux pas of the highest order. In the case of Attila the Hun, the first great conqueror from the land of Gog and Magog, the rebuff triggered a brutal chain reaction that led to the fall of a mighty empire.

In AD 441, six centuries after Alexander, Attila stood on the banks of the Danube opposite Belgrade, then called Singidunum, planning his attack. Europe was experiencing a time of unprecedented crisis; internal division was causing the Western Roman Empire to disintegrate, a power vacuum that barbarians from the East could exploit.

The Huns, described by the Roman soldier Ammianus Marcellinus as "a race savage beyond all parallel," were primitive nomads from Central Asia. They knew nothing of agriculture. They had no settled homes and no kings—until they moved into Eastern Europe, forcing out the indigenous peoples and settling in wary proximity to the Roman Empire, which occupied the lands across the Danube to the south.

As an important military stronghold, Singidunum guarded access to the Balkans, a region of Eastern Europe bordered by the Danube River to the north and the Adriatic Sea to the south, and was thus a primary military objective of the Huns. The settlement was attacked and leveled, and the Balkans were spared further destruction only when the unnerved Romans—who themselves had a long history of extorting subject peoples— in a stunning reversal of fortune agreed to pay tribute to the Huns. Suitably propitiated, Attila turned his armies eastward, where he waged war against Constantinople and the Eastern Roman Empire.

In 447 Attila was back at the doorway to the Balkans; the Romans had failed to pay the agreed-upon tribute. This time the people paid an appalling price as the Huns savaged both town and countryside in murderous retribution before a curious incident brought a temporary lull in the hostilities. A certain Honoria, older sister of the Western Roman Emperor Valentinian III, found herself in an unfortunate position and concocted a ruse that ultimately brought calamity to the Empire.

Not much is known of Honoria, and little is added by Sophia Loren's fulsome portrayal in the 1954 film *Attila*. Apparently Valentinian had decided to marry her off to a wealthy Roman senator who, it was said, was more gifted in his pockets than his visage. Aghast at the prospect, Honoria took the extraordinary step of sending her ring to Attila along with a plea for help. What she had in mind by this harebrained scheme will never be known, but Attila was rather taken with the idea. He immediately accepted what he considered to be a proposal of marriage. As for the dowry, Attila stipulated that Valentinian surrender fully one half of the lands of the Western Roman Empire, a quite impossible demand.

When word reached Valentinian of the impending addition to the royal family, he was quite understandably appalled. Only the intercession of the Queen Mother prevented him from having Honoria dispatched outright. She was instead exiled and disappeared from history, leaving Attila, as it were, standing at the altar and none too happy for it.

If he could not gain control of half of the Empire by marriage, he would conquer the whole of it by force. Attila set out to invade Gaul, sweeping across Europe as far as Orléans in central France—Paris having been spared, according to fond remembrance, by the fervent prayers of Saint Geneviève. After his advance was checked at the Battle of Châlons, Attila returned to Italy in 452 to claim his bride.

Pillaging their way down the Italian peninsula, the Huns ran out of steam at the River Po, their scorched earth campaign having left them without supplies to continue. Reluctantly, Attila retreated to his homeland and within a year would come to an ignominious end—dead, curiously, of a severe nosebleed while in a drunken stupor on the wedding night of his marriage to an Ostrogoth princess.

Attila, however, would continue to exercise profound influence on Europe, as the Huns were a primary force behind what historians call the Great Migration. In the fourth and fifth centuries, they expanded into Europe, attacking and forcing Germanic tribes westward, including the Goths, Saxons, Lombards and Franks, with further disastrous consequences for the Roman Empire.

Already in 410 the Visigoths under Alaric, having been driven across the Danube by the Huns, had triggered a succession of events that led to their rampaging along the Dalmatian coast and down through Italy, culminating in the first sack of Rome. The unthinkable had happened: For the first time in over nine centuries the Eternal City had fallen, sending shock waves throughout Christendom.

Another Germanic tribe, the Vandals, fled from before the Huns out of Pannonia westward along the Danube. Through a long, circuitous route taking half a century, they wrought havoc in Gaul. From there they crossed the Pyrenees into Hispania, and thence across the straits to the fertile lands of North Africa, where they besieged Hippo.

Inside the walls of the city, in the company of the emaciated, panic-stricken inhabitants, Saint Augustine lay dying. In *The City of God,* written during the earlier siege of Rome under Alaric, Augustine encouraged the faithful not to put their hopes and dreams in the earthly city that was passing away. Instead they should look beyond this transient world to the mystical, heavenly city of God—the New Jerusalem.

Mercifully, Saint Augustine did not live to see the fall of Hippo, whence the Vandals would later cross the Mediterranean to attack and pillage Rome in AD 455. The once mighty empire was broken apart, surviving in mutated form with the center of power migrating to the capital of the Eastern Roman Empire at Constantinople, the Eternal City retaining only her spiritual power.

The rule of a thousand years had come to an end, her destruction precipitated by invaders hailing from the mysterious land of Gog and Magog.

The Fortress of Klis

A full eight centuries would pass as Gog and Magog lay dormant. Then, suddenly, great danger arose once again from the East. The halcyon setting of the Adriatic resounded with the pounding hooves of battle horses as a great pursuit played out along the Dalmatian coast. King Bela IV of Hungary was fleeing for his life from the second of our conquering empires: the Mongols of Genghis Khan. These nomadic predecessors of the

Ottoman Turks also stormed out of Central Asia—the land of Gog and Magog.

A grandson of Genghis Khan, Batu Khan, was charged with the conquest of the West. In 1237 the Mongols invaded Russia, exterminating the forces sent against them, capturing Moscow and Kiev. The land was systematically decimated until all opposition was crushed and fully half of the population of Russia was dead. For nearly three centuries parts of Russia would remain under the subjugation of the Golden Horde—the name given to the western part of the Mongolian empire.

This medieval blitzkrieg was now bearing down on Europe, spreading terror and panic, devastating Poland, laying waste to Hungary and sweeping westward across the Pannonian Plain toward Vienna. King Bela IV, revered as one of the most famous kings of Hungary, dared to oppose the Mongols, with disastrous results.

After his armies were virtually annihilated at the Battle of Mohi in April 1241, Bela fled for his life. The Mongols, recognizing fortitude in a leader when they saw it, were determined to eradicate the potential threat once and for all. They pursued Bela across the Danube south into Croatia.

Bela took refuge in Zagreb, where his pleas for assistance went unheeded by the Western powers, including King Louis XIV of France, who was not at all troubled to see his Habsburg rivals in such a predicament. Seeing the meager defenses of Zagreb, Bela decided to escape to the Dalmatian coast, where he hid on the island of Rab. Reaching Zagreb, the Mongol forces promptly razed the city and marched toward the coast after him. Barely one step ahead of his pursuers, Bela fled by ship to the more heavily fortified town of Split.

As the Mongol army fought its way down the Dalmatian coast, devastating everything in its path, Bela lost his nerve and once again retreated offshore to the island of Trogir, from where he could escape to Italy by ship. Here the Mongol forces made a wrong turn: In the mistaken belief that Bela was hiding in the Klis Fortress above Split, they turned aside to attack it. They were in for a surprise, for the plucky defenders of the mountain rose quickly to the occasion, inflicting serious casualties and routing the attackers.

With the advance of the Mongol army checked at Klis, a portentous development would save Bela as well as the remainder of Europe. News arrived that the Grand Khan had died in Mongolia. Batu Khan, determined to have his say in the struggle over succession, at once wheeled his forces and returned to the East. The Mongols would never again launch an attack on the West and, once again, Europe was saved.

4

Battle of the Blood Drinkers

May 29, 1453, is a pivotal date in European history. After withstanding assaults from the lands of Gog and Magog for a millennium, Constantinople, capital of the Eastern Roman (Byzantine) Empire, was conquered by the Ottoman Turks.

The Turks were led by 21-year-old Sultan Mehmed II, known as the Blood Drinker for his fascination with peculiar means of torture. He wasted no time in launching an invasion of the Balkans. Mehmed set his sights on Wallachia, which controlled access to the mighty Danube River, from which the Holy Roman Empire launched attacks against the Ottomans.

Standing between his army and the wide-open Wallachian Plain was the Romanian prince Vlad III—or as he is better known, Vlad the Impaler, fictionalized as Dracula in Bram Stoker's 1897 novel of the same name. Death by impaling was particularly gruesome, as the poles often had rounded tips to avoid puncturing internal organs as they were driven through their victims' bodies, with the result that they would suffer sometimes for days.

Wallachia was the scene of many fierce battles as the Christian defenders attempted to repulse the Turkish invasion of Europe. Vlad III's father, Vlad II, was the ruler of Wallachia and a knight in the Order of the Dragon, dedicated to the defeat of the Ottomans. His surname was Dracul—or Dragon—and Vlad III would be known as Son of Dracul—or Dracula.

In 1442, through treachery, Vlad III became a prisoner of Sultan Murad II, held hostage to ensure that his father refrained from joining with the Hungarians against the Turks. Even though he was treated reasonably well and educated in philosophy, the Quran and the art of war, the years that Vlad III spent in captivity fueled his hatred for the Turks as well as a fiendish streak.

After six years of captivity, Vlad III returned home when his father was ousted as ruler of Wallachia and assassinated. In an act of brutality that likely helped turn him into a vicious killer, he learned that his older brother had been tortured, blinded and buried alive. He would spend the rest of his life attempting to secure his father's seat as well as fighting against the Ottoman Turks.

Vlad had a penchant for violence and put his Ottoman military training to use against his enemies, both foreign and domestic. According to one account, Vlad invited hundreds of local noblemen whom he viewed as potential rivals to a banquet. While they were supping he had his hapless guests stabbed before impaling their still twitching bodies on stakes. Later dozens of merchants who were once allied with the noblemen met the same gruesome fate. On another occasion, Vlad dined amidst a large number of defeated warriors writhing on impaled poles, reportedly dipping his bread in their blood.

When it came to savagery the Turks took a backseat to none. Vlad's only ally, Mihály Szilágyi, was captured by the Turks while traversing Bulgaria. His men were tortured to death and Szilágyi was killed by being sawed in half. In 1459 Sultan Mehmed II sent envoys demanding that Vlad pay tribute and contribute five hundred young men as recruits into the Ottoman army. To acquiesce would mean public acceptance of Wallachia as part of the Ottoman Empire. In reply, Vlad killed the emissaries by nailing their turbans into their skulls, thus setting the stage for war.

The cavalry of one thousand soldiers that Sultan Mehmed sent against Wallachia was ambushed in a narrow pass. In yet another demonstration of his appetite for sadism, he had the prisoners impaled, with their commander officer spiked on the highest beam to signify his rank. Now on a rampage, Vlad crossed the Danube and destroyed the Ottoman camps, laying waste the countryside. He wrote to an ally:

> I have killed peasants, men and women, old and young, who lived at Oblucitza and Novoselo, where the Danube flows into the sea. . . . We killed 23,884 Turks without counting those whom we burned in homes or the Turks whose heads were cut by our soldiers. . . . Thus, your highness, you must know that I have broken the peace.[1]

In response the Turkish Sultan, who was busy besieging a fortress in Corinth, ordered an army of eighteen thousand against the Wallachians. Vlad soundly defeated the Turks, only eight thousand of whom were said to have survived. His victory was celebrated throughout the Christian West and hailed by the Pope.

Such indignation could not be tolerated, and Mehmed led personally an invasion force to quell once and for all rebellious Wallachia and its impudent leader. He amassed an army of some ninety thousand men, including 120 cannons, which in numbers and armaments approached the force he had employed successfully against Constantinople.

Set against this formidable juggernaut were the meager thirty thousand men that Vlad could muster, most of whom were peasants and shepherds. Vlad failed in his bid for assistance from Hungary, despite offering to convert from Orthodoxy to Catholicism.

Bulgaria was the site of the clash of the two infamous rulers—each renowned for being quite literally bloodthirsty—in yet another chapter in the centuries-old strife between East and West in the Balkans.

The decisive battle that Mehmed sought eluded him. In a daring night attack, Vlad's forces infiltrated the Turkish camp, looking to dispatch the Ottoman Sultan. The assassination attempt failed, though some fifteen thousand of his soldiers were killed. The next day Mehmed continued his march on the Wallachian capital of Targoviste, only to be horrified and disgusted by the sight of thousands upon thousands of impaled Turks. It was too much even for the likes of one such as Mehmed, and he withdrew from the battlefield in disgust.

Vlad escaped capture and would continue his fight against his domestic foes until his death in 1476. There are conflicting reports of his death; according to one he died as he lived—in yet another battle attempting to stem the Muslim invasion of Europe.

Slave of God: Master of the World

Ah, Vienna!—that grand city of Europe and capital of the royal House of Habsburg, which ruled Austria for six centuries. Until the twentieth century the Austro-Hungarian Empire controlled central Europe as successor to the Holy Roman Empire. The city on the Danube was a bulwark against invasions from the East.

Long before the Communist era, Vienna stood guard at another border: protecting Western Christendom against attacking horsemen from the far regions of central Asia. It is here we meet our next conqueror from the land of Gog and Magog: Suleiman, Sultan of the Ottoman Empire, a fiercely aggressive Muslim empire centered in Anatolia.

Suleiman bestowed many titles upon himself, including "Slave of God: Master of the World." His begrudging admirers in Christendom called him Suleiman the Magnificent. He ruled over one of the most powerful empires in the history of the world at the time of its greatest reach. Suleiman's life and exploits were the stuff of legend: He drank from solid gold vessels, wore his silk robes only once before they were discarded and presided over a harem of hundreds of women. Such was the far-ranging reputation of the Sultan of Turkey that William Shakespeare paid tribute to him as a military prodigy in *The Merchant of Venice*.

Suleiman was bent upon fulfilling what all sultans considered their sacred duty: the subjugation of the infidel Christian West. That duty was especially urgent at a time when the tide had turned against the Muslims in Andalusia (modern Spain), where the fall of Granada marked the end of Islamic rule in the Iberian Peninsula. Accordingly, in his first year after acceding to the throne at age 26, Suleiman launched his campaign against Christendom.

At first he appeared unstoppable. In a lightning thrust into the Balkans, the Ottomans overran and destroyed Belgrade, the Serbian stronghold on the Danube. While Europe braced for the next blow, Suleiman unexpectedly swiveled south, turning his attention to the Mediterranean. There he unleashed an armada of four hundred ships against the island of Rhodes, reducing that bastion of the Knights Hospitaller and giving the Turks control of the eastern Mediterranean.

His southern flank secured, Suleiman resumed his invasion of the Balkans. By 1529 the Bulgarians and Albanians had fallen, followed by the defeat of Louis II of Hungary, laying open the valley of the Danube. Vienna was the last remaining barrier between the Ottomans and an increasingly terrified populace of Europe. Judging from the Ottoman advance thus far, slaughter, pillage, rape and slavery awaited those in the path of the Sultan's army.

In its most ambitious expedition to date, in the autumn of 1529—a little late, as we shall see—the Ottoman Turks surrounded Vienna with an army variously estimated between 120,000 and 300,000 men. Facing them behind the hastily reinforced walls of the city stood a motley garrison of some 16,000 luckless conscripts supported by an assortment of European mercenaries.

After nearly a century of unchecked expansion starting from before Suleiman's time, the Turks expected another quick, brutal victory. It was not to be. The defenders fought doggedly, even countering the Turks' efforts to bury explosives beneath the city walls by digging tunnels to intercept the charges. Just when it seemed the Viennese could hold out no longer, an intemperate European autumn set in, covering the tents of the unprepared troops of the Sultan with an unseasonably early snowfall.

Following one last all-out assault on the city walls, which was repulsed at great cost to both sides, Suleiman the Magnificent was for the first time in his storied career forced to admit defeat. Beset with disease and casualties, facing critical shortages of supplies and mired in snow and freezing mud, the Turks pulled up stakes and retreated before the full force of winter arrived.

The 1529 siege of Vienna proved to be the farthest reach of Ottoman expansion into Europe, as noted by Arnold Toynbee: "The failure of the first [siege of Vienna] brought to a standstill the tide of Ottoman conquest which had been flooding up the Danube Valley for a century past."[2]

The Battle of Vienna Redux

It was not the last that the Viennese would see of the Turks: After another century and a half of Ottoman aggression, punctuated by the storied naval battles of Preveza and Lepanto, the inhabitants of Christian Europe were again under dire threat when their "hereditary enemy" mounted one more attack on the sentinel of the Danube. The Battle of Vienna, on September 11 and 12 of 1683, was yet another pivotal event in European history—a date that radical Islamists would not forget, seeking revenge even far into the future with an infamous act of terrorism against the "Great Satan," the modern-day pinnacle of Christendom.

Determined to avenge the earlier humiliation, Ottoman commander Kara Mustafa oversaw extensive logistical preparations for the invasion, building and improving roads and bridges and amassing weaponry, including enormous Turkish bombard cannons. In his declaration of war, Sultan Mehmed IV left little to the imagination regarding the fate of the defenders of Vienna as he taunted the Holy Roman Emperor Leopold I:

> We order You to await Us in Your residence city of Vienna so that We can decapitate You. . . . We will exterminate You and all Your followers. . . . Children and adults will be equally exposed to the most atrocious tortures before being finished off in the most ignominious way imaginable.[3]

Eighty thousand Viennese along with Leopold got the message and abandoned the city, fleeing west to Linz. The worst fears of the remaining defenders would soon be confirmed. As the Sultan's army approached Perchtoldsdorf, a town in the vicinity of Vienna, the inhabitants surrendered the keys to the city, only to be slaughtered en masse and the few survivors driven into slavery. News of the atrocity sent a shock wave through Vienna's defenders, galvanizing their determination to resist the invaders.

Fortunately, the Viennese had time to strengthen the fortifications of the city, and even though the Turks were able to bring
their fearsome bombard cannons to bear, the walls stood firm.
The attackers then turned to the same stratagem employed in
the earlier assault on the city: underground mines. Thousands
of sappers set to work digging tunnels under the towering city
walls and preparing caches of explosives.

A pitched battle raged both above and underground amidst
a chaotic landscape. Wild Turks and Imperial troops, unfurling
either the crescent or the cross, were locked in mortal combat
outside the walls, while sappers for both sides clashed in the
dark confines of the tunnels. The daily carnage continued on
the blood-soaked ground as the attackers inched closer, cracking
through the Viennese fortifications. The walls were breached
in several places; it was only through desperate counterattacks
that the Viennese withheld the Turks.

After two months—their food supplies cut off—the Viennese
were starving. It was only a matter of days before the city would
be forced to capitulate, with consequences too dire to contemplate: The defenders learned that Kara Mustafa had already
ordered the execution of thirty thousand Christian hostages.
Little did the exhausted and terror-stricken Viennese garrison
suspect that their salvation was drawing nigh.

Deep into the night of September 11, sentries posted on the
walls looked up to see huge bonfires on Mount Kahlenberg
overlooking the city. It was the confederated troops of the Holy
Roman Empire, led by John III Sobieski, King of Poland, sig-
naling their arrival on the field of battle. In the early morning
hours of September 12, a mass was held on the heights for the
king and his nobles in preparation for the impending attack.

And not a moment too soon: The Ottoman sappers had
prepared a final, immense detonation under the city walls and
were sealing the tunnel to magnify the explosive force. At the

last moment, a brave Viennese "mole" succeeded in fighting his way through the lines and dashing into the tunnel to defuse the charge. Uncommon valor had become a common virtue.

The battle was soon joined. King Sobieski's forces, twenty thousand strong, swept down from the wooded heights in a devastating flank attack against the Ottoman hordes, who became the fateful target of the largest cavalry charge in history. It turned quickly into a rout; in less than three hours the battle for Vienna was over. Once again Western Christendom was saved.

The remnants of the defeated Turkish army abandoned the battlefield, retreating back across the Hungarian Plain, leaving behind tents, supplies and pillaged treasure, much of which is preserved in the museums of Vienna. Among the loot were sacks of coffee beans from which the Turks brewed an aromatic beverage that soon became the latest sensation in town—and the Viennese coffeehouse was born.

The battle for Vienna marked the end of Ottoman territorial expansion including three centuries of incursion into Western Europe. Over the next decade the Turks lost ground steadily, eventually losing control of Hungary and Transylvania. The Sultan was not pleased with this change of fortune. His Turkish commander Kara Mustafa paid for the ignominy with his life, suffering death by strangulation with a long silk cord, pulled taut by strong men on either side. His severed head was presented to the Sultan in a velvet sack, as was the custom.[4]

The Shot Heard Around the World

The Ottoman Empire struggled on for another two centuries before fateful events initiated a worldwide conflagration leading to 38 million casualties, including 17 million dead. It began in June 1914 when Archduke Franz Ferdinand, heir to the Austro-Hungarian throne, was shot to death in Sarajevo by a Serbian nationalist, one of many countrymen determined to see the land gain independence from Austria-Hungary.

Behind this movement for national sovereignty lay one of the most fateful dates in Serbian history: the Battle of Kosovo Field in 1389, where combined Serb forces attempted to turn back an Ottoman invasion of the Balkans. The brutal clash virtually wiped out both armies along with their commanders, Serbian Prince Lazar and Sultan Murad I.

The Turks, however, had an inexhaustible supply of replacements, while the Serbs, depleted after the long struggle against their enemies, could no longer adequately defend their territory. Consequentially, Bosnia and Herzegovina came to suffer under oppressive Ottoman rule until the late nineteenth century—a military occupation originating from the land of Gog and Magog.

Throughout their subjugation, the Serbian people held on to their determination not to be absorbed into another empire, even Austria-Hungary, which had liberated them from the Turks, and gave vent with a hail of bullets in Sarajevo.

The assassination of Archduke Ferdinand set into motion events that quickly spiraled out of control, leading to the First World War. At the conclusion of hostilities three years later, the maps of Europe and the Middle East were redrawn. The Great War saw the collapse of four empires: In Russia the Romanovs were defeated by the Bolsheviks; the House of Hohenzollern in Prussia and Germany was forced to abdicate; the Habsburg dynasty of Austria-Hungary fell; and the Ottoman Empire was dismantled.

The Great War also dealt a crushing blow to the European psyche, as suggested by one historian: "The real impact was moral. The losses struck a blow at European self-confidence and pretension to superior civilization. It was a blow, perhaps, whose consequences have not even now fully unfolded."[5] The lost "superior civilization" can be none other than Christendom, and the spiritual malaise in present-day Europe is the latter stage of the disintegration that began six centuries ago with the Ottoman conquest of Serbs in the fields of Kosovo. The weakness and poverty of faith have, in our day, opened the door to yet another invasion from Eastern lands.

Following the First World War, when the Ottoman Empire passed into history, Mustafa Atatürk brought Turkey into the Modern Age, abolishing the power of the Islamists and establishing a secular democratic state. But the ideal of a revived Muslim caliphate has never died; it grows stronger each year. With the ascension of the Islamist party along with the growing economic and military power of the Turkish state, the day may not be far off before the world witnesses yet another expansionist power rising out of the historic land of Gog and Magog.

Throughout part 1 we have seen devastation as well as the worldwide repercussions that follow, even centuries later, from invading malevolent forces—the same forces that will instigate the Final Battle at the end of time. In chapter 7 we discuss how the principal resistance to Gog and Magog comes not from the Middle East itself but from faraway lands—thus implying that the Arab nations of the region have largely been rendered ineffectual. We will now examine how the seeds of this disintegration, sown a century ago in the aftermath of the Great War, have borne catastrophic fruit.

PART 2

THE MIDDLE EAST AFLAME

5

The Muslim Savior

O my dear, they are making such a horrible muddle
of the Near East, I confidently anticipate that it will
be much worse than it was before the war. . . . It's
like a nightmare in which you foresee all the horrible
things which are going to happen and can't stretch
out your hand to prevent them.

—Gertrude Bell

The Middle East and neighboring lands were in a state of upheaval. Armies from Western countries, determined to conquer
and occupy in order to restore order to the region, engendered
feelings of humiliation and resentment among those who feared
subjugation of Muslim lands and pillaging of the natural resources. Hopes and expectations turned to the arrival of the
Mahdi, who according to Islamic eschatology would arise at
the end of days to defeat the enemies of Islam.

A shadowy figure emerged who claimed to be that divinely appointed leader—the redeemer of Islam who would establish a new Islamic state. Drawn to him by the thousands, Muslims took up arms against their own government, which they considered to be illegitimate and corrupt, a puppet of foreign powers. Advancing rapidly, the insurgents soon occupied large swaths of territory and proclaimed the revival of the caliphate—the pan-national Muslim government that fervent believers expect will eventually spread around the globe.

The setting for this aspiring Islamic state is not modern-day Iraq and Syria. Rather, it was Sudan, a couple of decades before the Great War, a time and place that bore a remarkable resemblance to current events in the Middle East. Like Iraq, Sudan was occupied by Western armies (British) that imposed rule through a proxy Sudanese government.

The Mahdi Army led by Muhammad Ahmad was marked by the same uncompromising brutality as ISIS is today: Strict sharia (Islamic) law was administered in lands under the army's control. Residents were given the choice between converting to Islam or death—often by beheading. Persecution of Christians in the Sudan under the Mahdi was particularly severe.

Sudan was nominally under the control of Egypt, which in turn was occupied by the British. After the Mahdi Army repulsed Egyptian forces sent against it, the British intervened directly. The distinguished General Charles Gordon, who had gained fame fighting for the Union Jack in far-flung conflicts, was chosen to lead the fight against the Mahdi Army.

A devout Christian, Gordon had traveled widely in the Holy Land and had discovered what he believed to be the authentic site of the crucifixion and burial of Jesus Christ. "Gordon's Calvary" remains an obligatory site on the itinerary of Protestant tours to Israel as an alternative to the Catholic and Orthodox site of the crucifixion located in the Church of the Holy Sepulcher.

Despite the fact that his ragtag army of Egyptian and loyal Sudanese soldiers was overmatched ten to one by the Mahdi Army, Gordon was confident of victory. Over his long career, after all, he had never lost a battle. Marching into the Sudanese capital of Khartoum in February 1884, he was immediately encircled and cut off by the 300,000-man Mahdi Army. Gordon did his best to muster the population and strengthen the city's defenses, but as the siege wore on it became apparent that he needed reinforcements.

When word reached England of his plight, there was a groundswell of demand that a relief column be sent to rescue the celebrated general and his troops. Before the long-delayed British column could reach Khartoum, however, the Mahdi Army swept over the city's ramparts and, in an orgy of destruction, slaughtered both soldiers and civilians indiscriminately. Gordon, by all reports, fought bravely to the end: A prisoner later recounted the fate of the Mahdi Army's most famous victim:

> Three black [Mahdist] soldiers were in the lead, one of whom [Slatin] recognized as a man named Shatta. . . . Shatta was carrying something wrapped in a bloody cloth. Slatin stood silent as they stopped in front of him, their faces triumphant. With a smile, Shatta undid the cloth while the crowd shouted. Slatin looked: it was Gordon's severed head. . . . "Is this not the head of your uncle, the unbeliever?"[1]

Six months later Muhammad Ahmad died, probably from malaria or typhus. His caliphate forged on though weakened by internal conflict. At long last, in 1895 the British launched an expedition led by Lord Kitchener to conquer Sudan and avenge the deaths of General Gordon and his men. Three years later at the Battle of Omdurman, the Mahdi Army was decimated by superior British firepower and faded into history.

The Desert Queen

Gertrude Bell was truly a woman extraordinaire—a British writer, linguist, archaeologist, explorer and spy who traveled widely throughout the Levant, the countries bordering the eastern Mediterranean in the early twentieth century. In those days a foreign woman crossing the desert sands was truly a rarity. With her trailing entourage of camels laden with wardrobe, full kitchen and bath, she was a sight to behold. Speaking fluent Arabic and Persian, Bell was welcomed by sheiks—who hailed her as the desert queen—into their tented compounds. Because of her extensive knowledge of the region, she was recruited in 1921 by His Majesty's Government to help draw the modern borders of the Middle East, unknowingly sowing the seeds of disintegration that the region would undergo in our day.

Since the sixteenth century, the Middle East had been ruled by the Turkish Ottoman Empire, but by the late nineteenth century the empire was greatly weakened and beset with political instability and outright revolt. Impressed by German industrial and military power, Turkey cast its lot with the Central Powers of Germany and Austria-Hungary during World War I in a desperate bid to regain its lost territories. The caliphate solemnly declared a military jihad against France, Russia and Great Britain.

The British seized the opportunity to expand their influence in the Middle East by fomenting rebellion against Ottoman rule in Arabia. The world's greatest maritime power was in the process of converting its ships from coal to oil, and was keen to safeguard a vital new source of petroleum. The Middle East was also strategically important as a land bridge between Europe and England's empire on the Indian subcontinent.

It was the stuff of Lawrence of Arabia—along with his collaborator Gertrude Bell. In return for waging guerrilla warfare against the Turks, the tribes of Arabia were promised their own kingdom after the war. Bell was proven right as she rued, "We people of the West can always conquer, but we can never hold Asia. That seemed to me to be the legend written across the landscape."[2]

In a word, when the Central Powers lost the war, Turkey lost its empire. Even before the cessation of hostilities, the British and French met secretly in Cairo to divide up the Middle East between them. The result was the Sykes-Picot agreement, which granted control of Iraq, Kuwait and Jordan to the British. The French were given Syria, Lebanon and southern Turkey. The parties deferred the thorny question of Palestine—then ruled by the British Mandate—for later.

Complicating matters was the growing influence of Zionists, who petitioned the British to be permitted to establish a homeland for the Jewish people. In 1917 Foreign Secretary Arthur Balfour issued a pronouncement declaring the British government's official support for a Jewish state in Palestine. The Balfour Declaration infuriated those who considered Palestine to be part of the anticipated pan-Arab nation. Muslims opposed the increased flow of Zionist immigrants into lands that had been theirs since Salah al-Din defeated the Crusaders in AD 1187.

Thus, through conflicting and irreconcilable commitments, the stage had been set for interminable conflict in the volatile region. The Arabs were promised a nation, yet Jerusalem—a land whose importance among Muslims is exceeded only by Mecca—would become the capital of a Jewish state carved from the midst of Arab lands. In addition, Lebanon would be categorized within Syrian territory as a state to be governed by Christian Arabs who had long endured second-class *dhimmi* status in the Middle East. And over all of this, Christian Europe would continue to hold sway: truly a recipe for disaster.

At the conclusion of the war, Bell was appointed Oriental Secretary and summoned to Cairo, where she assisted Winston

Churchill in finalizing the borders of the Middle East, in the process creating new states that arbitrarily cut across ethnic and tribal lands. For the most part, the leaders of these new states, chosen by the British and French, proved to be autocratic despots. Many viewed the resulting political instability as part of a Western plot to create disunity in the Arab world in order to maintain control over the oil wealth of the Middle East.

Clearly the "war to end all wars" had failed spectacularly in achieving its aim. As the century wore on, the entire manufactured edifice would totter, with both the oppressive political leadership and a radical Muslim insurgency feeding widespread resentment toward the region's infidel overlords.

The Muslim Brotherhood

Lurking behind much of the instability of the present-day Middle East is a movement seeking to establish a worldwide Islamic state. Borne out of Muslim fury at having their lands carved up and dominated by foreign infidels, from its beginnings in the 1920s the Muslim Brotherhood has promoted virulent xenophobia, directed predominately against Jews, Christians and other "unbelievers."

The Muslim Brotherhood has spawned numerous radical organizations, including Hamas and Egypt's Islamic jihad. It preaches Wahhabism, an extreme interpretation of Islam that originated during the eighteenth century in the wilds of Arabia. The Brotherhood advocates the use of violence to purge the "Muslim world" of infidels and envisions a pan-Islamic empire governed by sharia law.

The Muslim Brotherhood leader in Palestine, the Grand Mufti (Muslim legal expert) Amin al-Husseini, fomented riots against the British and organized the 1928 massacre of the Jews of Hebron. In a deadly precursor to today's Muslim suicide bombers, al-Husseini dispatched squads on suicide missions against the local authorities.

While in Germany during the Second World War, he played a leading role in encouraging Adolf Hitler to escalate his Final Solution extermination of Jews and other minorities. Al-Husseini created a division of Nazi Muslim soldiers who committed genocide in Bosnia, butchering more than 300,000 Jews, Serbian Christians and Gypsies.

A Palestinian Crematorium

In 1942 Hitler's Afrika Korps led by Erwin Rommel was pushing across Libya headed for the Suez Canal. The Germans were attempting to fulfill their Führer's scheme of conquering the Middle East and sweeping northward to link up with Army Group A in the Caucasus. As with their British foes' plan during World War I, the goal of the Axis armies was securing oil supplies, in this case the oil fields of Baku in present-day Azerbaijan in central Asia.

The Jewish community in the then-British Mandate was directly in the path of the Wehrmacht. According to a report in the Israeli newspaper *Israel Hayom* (*Israel Today*), Jewish sources were warned by a senior officer in the British Mandate police that al-Husseini was preparing to invade Palestine at the head of a Muslim Arab Legion force. The officer warned that "the mufti's plan was to build a huge Auschwitz-like crematorium in the Dothan Valley, near Nablus, where Jews from Palestine, Iraq, Egypt, Yemen, Syria, Lebanon, and North Africa would be imprisoned and exterminated, just like the death camps in Europe."[3]

The Mufti's plans were disrupted by British General Bernard Montgomery, whose Eighth Army defeated Rommel's Wehrmacht in the Libyan desert, putting an end to Hitler's designs on the Middle East—and al-Husseini's Jewish death chambers.

Despite the strong protests of Winston Churchill and others, after the war al-Husseini was permitted to escape unscathed from Germany and returned to Jerusalem, where he became a mentor to seventeen-year-old Yasser Arafat. Al-Husseini's young protégé would spend much of his life in violent struggle against the Jews.

Admirers of Arafat who focus on his reluctant participation in the Arab-Israeli peace talks ignore his legacy of terrorism:

> In fact, groups under Arafat's direct or indirect command— including Fatah, Black September, Tanzim and Al Aqsa Martyrs Brigade—were responsible for hundreds of bombings, hijackings, assassinations and other attacks, including the 1972 murder of 11 of Israel's Olympic athletes in Munich, the 1973 murder of the American ambassador to Sudan, Cleo Noel, and the 1985 hijacking of the Achille Lauro cruise ship (resulting in the murder of wheelchair-bound Leon Klinghoffer).[4]

Such is the legacy of the man who, jointly with Israel's Shimon Peres and Yitzhak Rabin, was awarded the Nobel Peace Prize in 1994 for his "efforts to create peace in the Middle East."

The Festering Sore

Gamal Abdel Nasser is a name that still evokes powerful emotions in the Middle East despite his mixed success as leader of the Arab Nationalist Movement. The former president of Egypt electrified Arabs by leading the first true revolt against colonialism. In 1956 he stunned Western powers by seizing control of the Suez Canal, provoking a combined attack by Great Britain, France and Israel. After United Nations resolutions forced the withdrawal of those countries, Nasser was hailed as the victor.

Bolstered by his growing reputation as the preeminent regional leader, Nasser set about addressing the greatest humiliation of the Arab world: the existence of a Jewish state in the heart of the Middle East. He founded the Palestine Liberation Organization and cobbled together a military alliance with Jordan and Syria for the purposes of commencing hostilities against Israel.

In May 1967 he demanded that the United Nations Emergency Force be withdrawn from the Sinai, where it served as a buffer between Israel and Egypt. Nasser then ordered a blockade of the Straits of Tiran, cutting off Israel's access to the Red Sea. He proclaimed succinctly the objective of the impending war: "the destruction of Israel."

Ringed by nearly half a million troops, more than 2,800 tanks and 800 aircraft, Israel faced imminent attack on all fronts by the armies of Egypt, Jordan and Syria. On the morning of June 5, the Israeli Air Force launched preemptive airstrikes against the Egyptian Air Force, destroying many of its planes on the ground. Over the next several days the Israel Defense Forces (IDF) struck in lightning succession, capturing the Gaza Strip and Sinai from Egypt, the West Bank from Jordan, and Syria's Golan Heights. Most significantly, Israel wrested control of East Jerusalem from the Arabs, including the Temple Mount and Western Wall.

The shame and indignity of the Arabs was compounded, as the hated Jews had now tripled the territories under their control, including the Dome of the Rock and the Al-Aqsa Mosque on the Temple Mount. In three years, Nasser would be dead of a heart attack. His successor, Anwar Sadat, undertook a final military effort that exceeded all previous attempts to wrest control of the Holy Land from the Israelis.

In October 1973 Egypt and Syria attacked on two fronts simultaneously. The surprise offensive, coming on the high holy day of Yom Kippur when much of the country was shut down, caught the IDF off guard. The Egyptian forces drove deeply into the Sinai as the Syrian Army swept across the Golan Heights.

With critical resupply provided by the United States, the Israelis finally managed to turn the tide and drive the Arab armies back deep into their own territory in some of the most intense tank battles in the history of modern warfare.

This last bitter defeat convinced Sadat that as long as the United States continued to provide financial and military assistance to Israel, the Arabs would never succeed in defeating the Jewish state. Desperate for economic assistance to rebuild his war-torn economy, Sadat accepted billions in American aid that came with a caveat: Egypt must turn her swords into plowshares.

The Egyptian president broke ranks with other Arab leaders and made a bold attempt at establishing peace in the Middle East. In 1977, to an astonished world and a rapturous Israeli public, Sadat flew to Ben Gurion Airport to meet with Israeli leaders. The ensuing negotiations led to the Camp David Accords in September of the following year, brokered by former-President Jimmy Carter. General agreement was reached on a framework to grant autonomy to the West Bank and Gaza. The status of Jerusalem, however, threatened to torpedo the talks and Carter judiciously left it off the table.

But the question of Jerusalem would not go away. It remained at the forefront of follow-up negotiations for years to come as both Palestinians and Israelis claimed the city as their capital. Displaying rank enmity for the Jewish people, Mahmoud Abbas, President of the Palestinian Authority—the government on the West Bank and Gaza—proclaimed defiantly, "Al Aqsa Mosque is ours. They [Jews] have no right to defile it with their filthy feet." With rhetoric unbecoming a head of state, Abbas encouraged aspiring terrorists, "We welcome every drop of blood spilled in Jerusalem. Every *shahid* [martyr] will be in heaven and every wounded person will be rewarded by Allah's will."[5]

Through the years the Muslim Brotherhood has evolved into a vast network of financial and business interests around the world, and has supporters and apologists along with front organizations working to influence Western governments. In recent years the secretive hand of the Muslim Brotherhood has been instrumental in founding and supporting Islamic terrorist groups around the world, including the Taliban, Al Qaeda, ISIS, Hamas and Boko Haram. These groups are fanatically committed to attacking Israeli and Western interests and ethnically cleansing Muslim lands.

The Covert War Continues

The Middle East and North Africa have been rent asunder by the Muslim Brotherhood and its surrogates—but nowhere has the upheaval been more evident than in the land of the Nile. In June 2012 the Muslim Brotherhood came to power in Egypt with the election of Mohamed Morsi to the office of president. His scant one-year tenure was marked by economic and security issues as well as food and energy shortages.

Morsi's forcing through of unpopular revisions to the Egyptian Constitution that were supported by the Muslim Brotherhood also sent protesters into the streets by the millions, forcing the military—the one stable institution in the country that enjoyed widespread respect—to intervene. In July 2014 Morsi was deposed by the military in a coup d'état.

A year later Defense Minister General Abdel Fattah al-Sisi was elected and sworn in as president of Egypt. In a sharp turn away from radicalism, Sisi declared the Muslim Brotherhood to be a terrorist group. Morsi and other leaders were arrested and charged with terrorism and plotting with foreign agents against Egypt.

Although accused of heavy-handed security crackdowns occurring during his watch, Abdel Fattah al-Sisi emerged as the foremost proponent of moderation in the Arab world—a title for which there are few challengers indeed. In a bomb-shell speech labeled as "courageous and historic" and delivered at Cairo's prestigious Al-Azhar University, Sisi's speech was a dagger at the heart of the extremist views of the Muslim Brotherhood.

Nothing short of astounding in a region inundated with extremism, Sisi declared during the conference, whose topic was "freedom of choice," that "the right to choose a particular faith, whether Christian, Jewish or Muslim is an inherent part of our religion."[6] Sisi argued that the Muslim world must confront the fanatic interpretations that were distorting Islam and were sweeping the Middle East.

The Muslim Brotherhood continued its covert war against Sisi, instigating a wave of terrorism in Egypt and the Sinai Peninsula. Natural gas pipelines, public transport and civilians have been targeted to undermine Egyptian internal security and bring down the government. In October 2015 a Russia-bound Metrojet aircraft taking off from Sharm el-Sheikh crashed in Egypt's Sinai Peninsula, killing all 224 people aboard. Investigators determined that a local affiliate of the jihadist group Islamic State (IS) had planted an explosive device onboard. Once again the secretive power of the Muslim Brotherhood struck a blow against foreign infidels.

The Shaking Off

Meanwhile in Israel, the end of the relative peace that the country enjoyed since the days of Anwar Sadat and Israeli Prime Minister Yitzhak Shamir can be traced to mobs of rock-throwing Arab youth in the towns of the West Bank and Gaza in December 1987. The first Palestinian *intifada* erupted as long-simmering resentment broke out into the open like the freeing of a captive who will not return to subjugation. The Arabic word means "to shake off," describing the attempt to throw off what was viewed as the oppressive yoke of Israel.

After a day or two of protests, things generally return to normal. Not this time: The strike continued day after day, with shops and schools remaining closed in solidarity with the uprising. While many citizens privately resented the continued disruption of their lives and means of livelihood, they dared not speak a word in public lest they be branded as hated collaborators.[7]

Since the outbreaks of the first, second and now third *intifada*, the return of calm to Israel's volatile borders—which Israelis desperately wish for—has proved elusive. The turmoil has spread throughout the region: With each passing year the Middle East has experienced a descent into chaos of ever increasing magnitude.

In the second decade of the 21st century, governments across the Levant and North Africa began falling like dominoes. Civil uprisings raging under the euphemism "Arab Spring" forced rulers from power in Tunisia, Libya, Egypt and Yemen; the leaders of other lands, including Iraq, Sudan and Syria, clung to power even as their respective states fragmented.

The Center Cannot Hold

Can we detect the passing by of the fiery red horse whose "rider was given power to take peace from the earth"? The ominous predictions of the apostle John in the book of Revelation (6:4) have undoubtedly inspired prophets through the ages, such as the more recent bleak futuristic vision of W. B. Yeats' "The Second Coming":

> Things fall apart; the centre cannot hold;
> Mere anarchy is loosed upon the world,
> The blood-dimmed tide is loosed, and everywhere
> The ceremony of innocence is drowned;

The best lack all conviction, while the worst
Are full of passionate intensity.

Yeats' poem does not purposely reflect Christian eschatology, as he had long abandoned the faith of his upbringing for a lifetime of dabbling in theosophy, spiritualism and the occult. He believed that history was cyclic and that the world would be engulfed in anarchy some two thousand years after the birth of Christ.

But whatever the inspiration behind "The Second Coming" and prophecies like it, visionaries are beginning to note present-day realities of the apostle John's warning: Spiritual malevolence is evident the world over. We have seen that a radicalized ideology is robbing the Middle East of peace by scoffing at calls for moderation and instead demanding the subjugation of humanity under harsh sharia law. We will now survey the violent history of this unyielding creed and the hidden stratagems used to mislead and disarm its opponents, as well as the tragic consequences for those considered to be "infidels" who fall under its sway.

6

Holy War
for the Promised Land

The concept of jihad, the perpetual state of war against infidels until the entire world comes under the rule of Islam and sharia law, is a religious obligation for Muslims. Muhammad was no stranger to warfare and bloodshed. He realized that his new religion would not spread beyond any single tribe until the strong family and clan allegiances found in Arabian society were broken. It was necessary, therefore, to convince his disciples to disregard their qualms about killing even family members who rejected the new "messenger of God":

> To overcome the age-old tradition of never spilling common blood was a considerable psychological victory. The new religion had no tribal boundaries. The son of Abd Allah Ubayy asked Muhammad's permission to kill his father for his "treachery" against Muhammad. It was necessary for him to be his father's

executioner; had anybody else killed him the son would have to seek blood vengeance.[1]

Muhammad demanded that his followers sever all family ties: The only "brothers" a believer was allowed were his fellow Muslims. Since many of the early Muslims were destitute, having left everything to follow him, they relied upon the time-honored tradition of robbing caravans in order to support themselves. The fighting skills honed in those early days would be put to use against any who resisted Muhammad's message. Christians are considered to be unbelievers because they reject Muhammad as the final revelation of God. They are also considered idolaters because they worship Jesus as God.

From AD 622 to 632, Muhammad and his early followers are recorded as having conducted no fewer than 81 military campaigns. The Koran is replete with commands to the faithful to fight for Allah:

> When the sacred months are over slay the idolaters wherever you find them. Arrest them, besiege them, and lie in ambush everywhere for them. . . . Prophet, make war on the unbelievers and the hypocrites and deal rigorously with them. Hell shall be their home: an evil fate.
>
> Repentance 9.5, 73

After Muhammad's death in 632, Abu Bakr, the first caliph or successor to Muhammad, galvanized his followers into a formidable fighting force that fanned out across the desert bent on conquest. They were soon in Transjordan gazing at the bastion of Christianity in the Middle East, the land of Palestine. The Byzantine Empire in the Holy Land was exhausted by a costly struggle with Persia and could offer little resistance to the invaders. In 638 Jerusalem surrendered without a struggle.

The Muslim warriors then turned their sights toward Egypt. After several decades they had conquered all of North Africa and crossed over into Spain. The loss to the Christian landscape was incalculable: The very cradle of the Church's early life, and home to most of the Church Fathers, was irretrievably lost. Three of the most venerable and important Christian "sees"—Jerusalem, Antioch and Alexandria—were captured. The Christian communities in Egypt and North Africa, the home of such saints as Antony of the Desert, Cyril of Alexandria, Athanasius, Augustine and Cyprian of Carthage, were overrun.

It seemed that nothing could stop the Muslim armies as they conquered the Iberian Peninsula and marched into France. They would, however, finally meet their match in one of the decisive battles of history. In 732 the armies of Islam were turned back by Charles Martel in the Battle of Tours.

It took another eight centuries before the last vestiges of Muslim rule were expelled from Spain after the capture of Granada in 1492. By that time Europe was coming under assault from the East, as the Ottoman Turks advanced as far as Vienna—but we already know the end of that story.

The House of War

According to Muslims the world is divided into two spheres of influence. The first is the *Dar al-Islam,* or the "House" (territory, lands) of those who submit to Allah. The second is the *Dar al-Harb,* the "House of War"—also called the "House of the West." This refers to lands that are not Muslim. They are unclean by definition and remain impure until becoming part of the House of Submission.

Those living in the Dar al-Harb face a stark choice: Either convert to Islam or be killed. Those who are "people of the book" (Christians and Jews) are generally tolerated so long as

they pay the *jizya* (religious tax) and abide by numerous prohibi-
tive restrictions that in effect render them second-class citizens.

The *jizya* is often presented today as an innocuous formality.
In reality the tax was often crippling—demanding as much as
50 percent of one's income—and was responsible for destroying countless families. The tax functioned as a lucrative extor-
tion racket, which was practiced down through the centuries
as part of the brutal Ottoman rule over Christians, Jews and
other non-Muslims.

In Armenia, the wives and children of those who were unable to pay the *jizya* were condemned to slavery. The Serbs of
Europe were particularly hard hit and often had to surrender
their children to satisfy the collector. The children were then
converted to Islam and trained as jihad warriors (often part of
the elite corps of Janissaries) to attack Christian lands. This
taxation enabled Islam over a period of time to make inroads
into populations that wanted nothing to do with it.

The legal status of unbelievers in Muslim lands is that of
dhimmis or "protected minorities"—a so-called protection
that is more accurately described as a license to oppress. The
second caliph, Omar bin al-Khattab (634–644), laid out what
has come to be known as the "Conditions of Omar"—or restrictions put upon unbelievers in Muslim lands. Under pain
of death or enslavement, the *dhimmis* agreed to a long list of
demands, including:

- The erection or repair of churches and synagogues
  which did not exist during the pre-Muslim period was
  prohibited. . . .
- They were not to employ a Muslim in their service, and
  in partnerships with non-Muslims they were restricted to
  the role of the "silent" rather than the trafficking partner.

- Protected subjects [*dhimmis*] were to honor the Muslims and stand in their presence. They could not deceive or strike them.
- They were to accommodate Muslim travelers for three days. . . .
- They were not to resemble Muslims in their clothing or hairdressing. The Jews were to wear yellow clothes, girdles, and hats, the Christians, blue. . . .
- Entry into bathhouses was only to be authorized when a special sign was worn on the neck which would distinguish them from Muslims. . . .
- They were forbidden to carry arms.
- They were not to ride on horses or mules but only on asses, and then on packsaddles without any ornaments, and not on saddles. They were to ride sidesaddle.
- Their houses were not to be higher than those of the Muslims. . . .
- They were not to raise their voices in their churches or be seen in public with crosses.
- They were not to be employed as government officials or in any position which would grant them authority over Muslims.
- The property of the deceased was to belong to the authorities until the heirs proved their right to it according to Islamic law.[2]

Due to Western influence in the Middle East during the twentieth century, restrictions imposed upon unbelievers largely disappeared. In the wake of the Arab Spring and the resurgence of Islamic radicalism, however, Christians and other minorities throughout the Muslim world are once again being made subject to *dhimmi* proscriptions. Crosses and Bibles are considered "polytheistic" provocations that can trigger harsh reprisals. Churches are burned, bombed or denied permits to build or renovate, and Christians who speak openly about their faith are accused of proselytizing or blaspheming—both of which are capital offenses.

Muslims believe that Islam is destined to rule the earth as the final and superior revelation of God. If possible, Muslims should not be ruled by non-Muslims. Moreover, any land that was once conquered by Muslims must forever be considered to be Muslim even if it reverts to the control of the infidels. In 1985 Iran's Ayatollah Khomeini—the architect of the Islamic revolution—commissioned a map that divided the world into Dar al-Islam and Dar al-Harb. Countries such as Spain and the Balkans, which have not been under Islamic control for centuries, were included as part of the Muslim sphere of influence.

The entire Levant including the Holy Land was considered to be within the realm of Dar al-Islam. For Muslims the State of Israel is a "cancerous tumor" in the midst of Arab lands: a reversal of history resulting in the humiliating rule of Jews over Muslims. The outrage is compounded by Jewish control over Jerusalem, which holds the Haram esh-Sharif (the Temple Mount) and Al-Aqsa Mosque, the latter of which is the third holiest site in Islam. Thus it is the duty of Muslims everywhere to reverse this intolerable state of affairs and return the infidels to their rightful *dhimmi* status.

Islamic teaching suggests that the final rule of Allah on earth will be established after the last Jews are killed. In the *Hadith*—the authoritative Islamic traditions of the prophet—we read: "Allah's Messenger (may peace be upon him) said: 'You will fight against the Jews and you will kill them until even a stone would say: "Come here, Moslem, there is a Jew hiding himself behind me, kill him."'"[3]

So deep is their aversion that many Muslims cannot bring themselves to utter the word *Israel*. To do so would be to grant the Jewish state a reality they wish to deny. Instead they refer to the "Zionist entity," which for them is an artificial imposition upon Arab lands.

Palestinians are taught to hate Jews at an early age. Speaking at the United Nations, Israeli ambassador Danny Danon urged the Security Council to take steps against an "incitement that fuels terror." Danon held up a card with a diagram of human anatomy entitled "How to Stab a Jew." Danon said: "When a Palestinian child returns from school and opens [sic] the TV, he doesn't see Barney or Donald Duck, he sees murderers portrayed as heroes. When he opens a textbook, he doesn't learn about math and science, he's being taught to hate."[4] The diagram is used by the Palestinian Authority to teach children in elementary schools: "Palestinian leaders have established an incubator to raise children as terrorists."[5]

In a televised interview Grand Ayatollah Ahmad al-Baghdadi, the leading Shia cleric of Iraq, claimed that it was impossible for Islam and the rest of the world to coexist peacefully. According to the Ayatollah, whenever possible Muslims are obligated to strive forcibly to conquer non-Muslims by what he termed "offensive jihad." He berated his interviewer for suggesting that Islam does not teach such intolerance:

> If they are people of the book [Jews and Christians] we demand of them the jizya—and if they refuse, then we fight them. That is if he is Christian. He has three choices: either convert to Islam, or, if he refuses and wishes to remain Christian, then pay the jizya [and live according to *dhimmi* rules]. But if they still refuse—then we fight them, and we abduct their women, and destroy their churches—this is Islam! . . . Come on, learn what Islam is, are you even a Muslim?[6]

Lying to Advance the Truth

Such pronouncements often appear only in the Arabic media, with sanitized versions found in English language publications. It is difficult to ascertain what is actually happening in the Middle East and other Muslim lands because Muslims believe they are permitted to give false or misleading statements to unbelievers. Thus Muslims might give one impression to infidels while saying something quite different to fellow believers.

In June 1991 Imam (preacher) Siraj Wahhaj became the first Muslim to deliver the opening prayer to the U.S. House of Representatives. The prominent Muslim spokesman and leader of the Muslim Alliance in North America quoted from the Koran and offered an articulate appeal to the Almighty to guide American leaders and "grant them righteousness and wisdom."

It turns out the imam's invocation was an illustration of the Islamic doctrine of *taqiyya*, whereby Muslims are permitted to deceive unbelievers if it will advance the cause of Islam. The Koran expressly states: "And they [the disbelievers] schemed, and Allah schemed [against them]: and Allah is the best of schemers" (Koran 3:54).

Clearly Wahhaj, an American-born citizen, intended to portray Muslims as gracious fellow believers in God who are supportive of the United States government. As one admiring observer noted: "The prayer was so eloquent and poignant, and it was fitting that the Nation's Masjid during Ramadan is helping lead an effort of changing the perceptions of Muslims in the United States of America."[7]

A year later, however, as Daniel Pipes notes, Wahhaj

> articulated a rather different vision of his gracious and moderate invocation in the House. If only Muslims were more clever politically, he told his New Jersey listeners, they could take over the United States and replace its constitutional government

with a caliphate: "If we were united and strong, we'd elect our own emir [leader] and give allegiance to him. . . . [T]ake my word, if 6–8 million Muslims unite in America, the country will come to us."[8]

Wahhaj has also spoken approvingly of the severe punishments dictated by sharia law:

> If Allah says 100 strikes, 100 strikes it is. If Allah says cut off their hand, you cut off their hand. If Allah says stone them to death, through the Prophet Muhammad, then you stone them to death, because it's the obedience of Allah and his messenger—nothing personal.[9]

Despite the fact that most Americans find such Koranic punishments to be offensive and contrary to our system of government, Wahhaj has boasted: "Islam is better than democracy. Allah will cause his *deen* [Islam as a complete way of life], Islam to prevail over every kind of system, and you know what? It will happen."[10]

Four years after giving the invocation on Capitol Hill, Siraj Wahhaj would gain notoriety by becoming a character witness for the "blind sheik" Omar Abdel-Rahman, who was convicted of conspiring to bomb New York's World Trade Center in 1993. Though never charged, Wahhaj was identified by the lead U.S. attorney in the case as one of a number of "unindicted persons who may be alleged as co-conspirators."[11]

Wahhaj has been identified by Stephen Schwartz, executive director of the Center for Islamic Pluralism, as a prominent Muslim hatemonger: "He's the No. 1 advocate of radical Islamic ideology among African-Americans. His stuff is very appealing to young Muslims who are on a radical path."[12] In a report on radical Islam in America's prisons, Schwartz reported that Wahhaj's writings are available in prison libraries and are influential in radicalizing young Muslims behind bars.

ISIS' Ethnic Cleansing

Many fervent Muslims are drawn to a new terrorist organization that has burst upon the scene, and which takes jihad to new levels of barbarism. In the space of less than two years ISIS has seized control of territory in Iraq and Syria that is the size of Great Britain, raking in hundreds of millions of dollars from oil fields. An estimated twenty thousand radicalized Muslim youth from Europe and other Western countries have flocked to ISIS-controlled areas to take part in the jihad.

This growing fanaticism has turned the Middle East into a killing ground for "unbelievers." Writing in the *Telegraph,* retired Bishop of Canterbury Lord Carey warned that the volatile region is undergoing murderous ethnic cleansing on an unprecedented scale:

> [Christians] are the most vulnerable and repeatedly targeted victims of this conflict. . . . A hundred years after the Armenian and Assyrian genocide, in which over a million Christians are estimated to have been killed by Ottoman Muslims, the same is happening today in the form of an ethnic cleansing of Christians in the region. Christians have been crucified, beheaded, raped, and subjected to forced conversion. The so-called Islamic State and other radical groups are openly glorifying the slaughter of Christians.[13]

As ISIS spreads across Iraq and Syria, religious minorities find themselves in the crosshairs, sending them fleeing by the tens of thousands. The London *Express* reports that Christians are being martyred by ISIS militants at a rate of one every five minutes:

> Believers are often singled out, tortured and faced with the brutal choice of converting to Islam or being slaughtered, according to Christian Freedom International. Those who refuse to comply have reportedly had their limbs cut off or have been crucified.[14]

Christian Freedom International reports that there have been more Christian martyrs in the 20th and 21st centuries than in the previous 19 combined. Christian churches are being desecrated, stripped of their valuable relics and used as torture chambers where believers are forced to choose between converting to Islam and death.

"A Genocide of Christians" reads the *Israel National News* headline, a publication in a country that knows more than most the meaning and horror of genocide. The article discusses a report by the Justice and Peace Commission of the Bishops of Dublin, which reveals: "Every year, more than 100,000 Christians are murdered just because of their faith. This means that 11 Christians are murdered every hour."

Tragically, the article describes how the systematic killing of Christians in the Middle East and other Muslim countries continues unabated as "the West sleeps." This is in large part due to the moral poverty of the West, which having long abandoned its spiritual heritage lacks the will to defend Christians and confront the evil forces that are savaging them.

Among believers in the United States, the most powerful Christian nation on earth, another dynamic is hampering concern for the plight of their brethren in the Middle East. Many Christians in Arab lands are members of strange-sounding and unfamiliar church affiliations, such as Coptic, Chaldean, Armenian, Melkite and Orthodox (Catholics are called "Latins").

Because of doctrinal differences, many evangelical and charismatic/Pentecostal Christians frankly doubt if members of such churches are genuine Christians. While Americans live in what much of the world considers to be the lap of unimaginable luxury, thankful for possessing the "true" faith, churches in the Middle East that we know little about are undergoing relentless persecution for refusing to renounce their faith in Christ.

In Middle Eastern towns and cities, Islamists are displacing, killing or forcibly converting Christians. Taking a page from the evil playbook of the Nazis who painted the Star of David on the homes of Jews, the jihadists are marking the homes of Christians with the letter N (for the Arabic word for Christian, i.e., a follower of the Nazarene).

Churches throughout areas under ISIS control have been demolished, with their congregants massacred or driven from their homes. The Islamists, states the article, "proclaim that they will not stop until Christianity is wiped off the face of the earth."

Having lost their homes and livelihoods, the displaced Christians have few options. They dare not show up at the United Nations refugee camps for fear of their lives: Christian refugees are routinely ejected—or worse—by the Muslim majority.

The former Archbishop of Canterbury expressed concern over their plight: "The frustration for those of us who have been calling for compassion for Syrian victims for many months is that the Christian community is yet again left at the bottom of the heap." He criticized a policy that

> inadvertently discriminates against the very Christian communities most victimized by the inhuman butchers of the so-called Islamic State. Christians are not to be found in the UN camps, because they have been attacked and targeted by Islamists and driven from them. They are seeking refuge in private homes, church buildings and with neighbors and family.[15]

Persecuted Christians seeking asylum in the United States face a Catch-22: They are required to apply through the United Nations—but they fear to enter the UN camps to be processed.

Should they attempt to flee across the Mediterranean to Europe, danger follows them. In April 2015 Italian authorities arrested fifteen Muslims for throwing fellow refugees off a boat to their deaths when they were discovered to be Christian.

Those who survive the trip and reach Europe soon find themselves threatened by Muslim migrants. Syrian Christian refugees in Sweden reportedly were forced from their asylum house after their Muslim compatriots banned them from the communal areas and demanded that they hide their crosses. Similarly, Pakistani Christians in refugee centers in the Netherlands report being bullied and threatened by Muslim migrants.

Europe and the United States are viewed as the last refuge for those displaced by the tumult in Muslim lands. Many of the migrants, however, bring with them a religious ideology that is antithetical to Christianity. Even more alarming are concerns that saboteurs hidden among the flood of migrants constitute a Trojan horse seeking to undermine and destroy Western society—a fear that would be borne out on the streets of Paris and in San Bernardino.

We will now examine this migrant tsunami that threatens to engulf Europe—and the United States.

7

Camp of the Saints

Churches by the thousands sparsely attended or shuttered, a continent dotted with old disused monasteries—imposing relics of another day when a vibrant Church built abbeys and convents across Europe, filled with young seminarians and nuns sent by pious families to train for service. Now they serve as forlorn memorials to the enfeebled Christendom so brilliantly depicted in Jean Raspail's apocalyptic novel.

Originally published in 1973, *Le Camp des Saints* would prove to be so remarkably prescient—and controversial—that not only would it be a bestseller on both sides of the Atlantic, but four decades later, as events proved the author correct, the novel would return to the top of the list. Raspail paints a dismal portrait of the twilight of an emasculated Western Europe, devoid of political resolve and impoverished of spirit, being overwhelmed by an alien culture from the East.

The Camp of the Saints begins in Calcutta, where an Indian "wise man" incites his impoverished followers to make a mass migration to Europe to conquer the kingdom of the "little Christian god." He regales them with a loose quotation from the book of Revelation: "The nations are rising from the four corners of the earth, and their number is like the sand of the sea. They will march up over the broad earth and surround the camp of the saints and the beloved city" (see Revelation 20:8–9).

Inspired by their leader the crowd moves en masse to the docks, where they manage to commandeer a dilapidated four-stack liner. Emboldened by their success, mobs up and down the Ganges imitate their example until a fleet of one hundred rusted ships has pulled anchor, sailing for the promised land of Europe.

When word reaches Europe, there is panic in the streets at the prospect of a million refugees flooding the continent. The fears of the populace are assuaged by the cultural elite, the media and the government, themselves under the sway of a charismatic journalist who urges acceptance of the "Last Chance Armada" in the name of Christian charity, love and the brotherhood of man. The leaders of Europe's churches call for welcoming the refugees; this includes the Catholic Church, headed by—get this—a Brazilian Pope.

Unconvinced, masses of Frenchmen flee the coastal areas as the fleet of rundown ships approaches. What follows is a slow descent into madness as the immigrants scoff at calls to assimilate, choosing instead to loot, rape and bring about the destruction of the Christian citadel of Europe. Predictably, critics dismissed the novel as "racist, xenophobic and paranoid."

The Floodgates Open

Raspail has had the last word. Europe is facing its worst refugee crisis in half a century as migrants from Muslim lands flood in by the hundreds of thousands—soon to be millions. It is true that many of the arrivals are seeking only an opportunity for life free from violence and terror. Many others, however, refuse to embrace the culture and values of their new land. Instead they cling to a harsh, intolerant ideology that seeks to supplant the continent's Christian heritage.

With bags in hand and children hoisted on their shoulders, the migrants are flooding through southern Europe's porous borders. Others brave the perilous sea voyage across the Mediterranean packed into dangerously overloaded vessels called "death boats" because of the high fatality rate.

The migrants are seeking to escape the violence and devastation in the Middle East and North Africa—conflicts that have left hundreds of thousands dead while displacing more than eleven million. Most are heading for the more affluent western and northern European countries—and their southern counterparts were initially happy to oblige. Greece allowed the refugees to pass through on their way north to Macedonia, which, overwhelmed by the determined hordes, moved them quickly through their country to the border with Hungary.

Already 20 percent of the population of France is foreign born—most from Muslim North Africa or Middle Eastern descent. Norway is not far behind with 16 percent of its population swearing allegiance to the prophet. Germany is bracing for record numbers of asylum-seekers, drawn by the country's extensive and generous network of social services. And those arriving are only the tip of the iceberg: Each refugee can be expected to arrange for up to eight relatives to join him, as they are entitled to do if granted refugee status. This could add more than seven million migrants—or nearly 10 percent to Germany's population of eighty million as a result of the 2015 influx alone. The financial strain that these migrants are placing on the economy has led to anti-refugee protests as well as increasing numbers of arson attacks and other "hate crimes" against migrants and asylum facilities.

In Sweden the situation is even more acute, with Muslims already constituting 22 percent of the population. Cities like Malmo have been radically transformed into Islamic enclaves where reportedly even the police do not dare venture. With a birthrate more than double that of native Europeans, across the continent, the favored name of male babies is rapidly becoming Muhammad.

Applauded in 1989 for helping to break the Iron Curtain by opening its border with Western Europe, these days Hungary is singing a different tune. With limited resources and swamped with migrants, the country raced to complete a border fence to keep refugees out. Initially criticized for betraying "European values," as the crisis wore on more and more countries began emulating Hungary by building border fences of their own.

Still they came by the thousands and hundreds of thousands, scrambling to find alternate routes to northern Europe. U.N. High Commissioner for Refugees António Guterres calls it "a tragedy without parallel in the recent past." The *Washington Post* notes that there is little hope that the migrants will be returning to their devastated homelands anytime soon, "presenting the international community with a long-term crisis that it is ill-equipped to address and that could prove deeply destabilizing, for the region and the wider world."[1]

As the months passed German Prime Minister Angela Merkel was forced to acknowledge that her original estimate of 800,000 new migrants entering the country in 2015—itself double the 2014 number—was spectacularly off. Her nation expected to see up to 1.5 million refugees before the year was out.

A Risky Gambit

Faced with an aging demographic, northern Europe hoped to use migrants from the Middle East and North Africa to fill a growing need for skilled labor. The new arrivals, however, often lacked the necessary skills for Europe's high-tech industries. In the Netherlands, only 10 percent of immigrants have completed higher education or attended a university. As a result, unemployment in the Moroccan and Turkish communities is up to three times that of the native Dutch people. Significant numbers of non-Western immigrants receive some form of social welfare.

A Turk living in Germany is two or three times more likely to be unemployed than a German. Many are dependent on public housing and the generous social benefits for food and clothing. German economist Bernd Raffelhüschen noted that a high percentage of the refugees are low-skilled workers: "That number will now come up to 1.5 million people . . . about 70 percent of whom are also unqualified."[2] He predicted that "massive tax increases" would be inevitable to pay for the social programs for the migrants. Instead of having the labor shortage alleviated by new workers, many Germans will now be forced to work well into their seventies.

An increasingly skeptical German public slowly came to realize that disconcerting numbers of refugees—like those of Raspail's novel—show little interest in adapting to Western culture traditionally informed by Christian principles such as freedom of speech and religion, and the rule of law. The trails of garbage and refuse left behind by some refugees were an affront to the famously ordered Teutonic mindset. More serious was the burgeoning violence as mass brawls erupted in the migrant camps along with reports of rape and sex slavery as well as increasing crime rates in the local communities.

Indeed some of the migrants consider Europe's social benefits to be the infidel's payment of *jizya* tax. For them it is proof of Islam's superiority and inevitable domination of the Christian West.

Allegiances in Middle Eastern culture are centered around one's family, and beyond that in widening circles to one's clan, as expressed by the old Bedouin proverb: "I against my brothers. I and my brothers against my cousins. I and my brothers and my cousins against the world." Nepotism is rife in the Arab world, where available jobs go first to one's immediate family, next to one's relatives, and so on.

It is an utterly foreign concept for many Muslims to work for the benefit of unrelated strangers—especially infidels—in order to prop up Europe's welfare states. In the words of Daniel Greenfield:

> Why should 23-year-old Mohammed work for four decades so that Hans or Fritz across the way can retire at 61 and lie on a beach in Mallorca? The idea that Mohammed would ever want to do such a thing out of love for Europe was a silly fantasy that European governments fed their worried citizens.[3]

More likely Mohammed will choose to work "off the books" in the traditional Arab way so that his money goes to support his own family. By thus doing he helps ensure that what Greenfield calls "the great gamble of the European welfare state" will collapse upon itself.

Those who have done the math are pessimistic, as expressed by one commentator: "It appears too late for Christian Europe to recover. Indeed, all signs suggest the next 25 to 50 years will see the inevitable displacement and Islamization of Europe's Christian population."[4]

Three decades after *The Camp of the Saints*, in a 2004 essay Raspail expresses his deep pessimism at the state of affairs in Europe:

> I am convinced that the fate of France is sealed, because "My house is their house" (Mitterrand), inside "Europe whose roots are as much Muslim as Christian" (Chirac), because the situation is moving irreversibly towards the final tumble in 2050 which

will see French stock amounting to only half the population of the country (the oldest members), the remainder composed of black Africans, North Africans and Asians of all sorts from the inexhaustible reserve of the Third World, predominantly Islamic, understood to be fundamentalist jihadists, this dance is only the beginning. France is not the only concern. All of Europe marches to its death.[5]

Hijra: Jihad by Other Means

Western viewers were astonished to see a shocking video taken of a train full of refugees heading to Germany, which, instead of gratitude, revealed open hostility as they openly cursed their new hosts:

> "Allahu Akbar!" (Allah is greater).
>
> "May Allah make orphans out of their children," cries out the man in the train as the crowd replies "Amen."
>
> "May Allah make it difficult on their women."
>
> "Allah give victory to Islam everywhere."
>
> "Allah give victory to our brethren in Palestine."
>
> "Allahu Akbar, Allahu Akbar . . . there is no god but Allah and the martyr is beloved by Allah."[6]

Other refugees at European train stations were filmed contemptuously throwing unopened food and water containers onto train tracks because the donations were discovered to have come from the Red Cross.

While Westerners find such behavior incomprehensible and highly offensive, the actions of these Muslim refugees are rooted in a little-known Islamic doctrine of *Hijra*. In her book *Refugee Resettlement and the Hijra to America*, Ann Corcoran describes "jihad by migration":

95

Hijra remains the model to this day for jihadists who seek to populate and dominate new lands. Their migrations are not for the purpose of assimilating peacefully in a new host nation, adopting as their own its traditions and legal systems. Rather, Mohammed's followers, in keeping with the example established by their prophet, are driven first to colonize and then to transform non-Muslim target societies—whether through violent means or via stealthy, pre-violent ones favored by the Muslim Brotherhood when it is not powerful enough to use violence decisively. . . . By aiming very explicitly at changing the demographics, legal systems and governments of such infidel states in an incremental process, the civilization jihadists advance their ultimate objective—global submission to Sharia and the reestablishment of a caliphate to rule according to it.[7]

The tidal wave of refugees threatens to turn the motto of the European Union, "Unity in diversity, freedom, peace, and solidarity," on its head. When the member states adapted the rallying cry, no one could have imagined that diversity would ultimately mean absorbing up to fifty million migrants over a period of decades.

The more extremist Muslim migrants view themselves as the ambassadors of a dominant religion destined to rule over unbelievers. Journalist Daniel Greenfield describes the all-too-common lack of thankfulness on the part of some migrants while enjoying the generous social benefits provided by benefactors, including one refugee who "hasn't worked, paid or thanked anyone for any of it":

And why would he? He's entitled to it by virtue of his superiority as a Muslim and our inferiority as infidels. There is no sense of gratitude. Only constant demands as if the people who drove out their own Christians and Jews have some moral claim on the charity of the Christians and Jews of the West.[8]

The continent is reaping the bitter fruit of its utopian fantasy that all religions are inherently equal—or equally pointless—and thus Europe has nothing to fear by admitting large numbers of Muslims, who will surely be impressed with the high standard of living and aspire to emulate their hosts. Significant numbers of migrants, unable and unwilling to assimilate, are venting their rage through criminal activity. It is the soldiers of this increasingly lawless minority faction of Muslims who

> butcher British soldiers or Dutch artists on the streets of their own hometowns, "groom" tens of thousands of little British girls and rape tens of thousands of Scandinavian women, shoot up with military rifles French, Belgian, Danish and German citizens, toss hand grenades in Sweden and petrol bombs in France, blow up commuter-stuffed trains in Spain and trash bins in Italian high schools, set up terror-ruled Sharia "no-go" zones all over Europe, decapitate in Syria, and now riot, attack ferries, trains and buses, pull people out of their cars by their hair, and murder Nigerian Christians at sea and Sicilian grandparents on land.[9]

A Third Battle for Vienna

The flood of migrants from the East shows no sign of abating. Crowds of fist-pumping young Arabs shouting Islamic slogans is causing some to draw parallels with historic incursions of Muslims streaming from Turkey to extend the Muslim caliphate into Europe. Could Europe be witnessing a third invasion of the continent following in the footsteps of historic onslaughts of the gates of Vienna?

Bat Ye'or, author of *Eurabia: The Euro-Arab Axis*, argues that the march of the "universal Caliphate" into Europe is well underway:

It has set itself up as the protector of the Muslim immigrant masses in the world and requires that they remain firmly anchored in the Islamic traditions of the Koran and Sunna, following the Sharia laws while the Europeans are called upon to abandon their historic values and even their identity condemned as Islamophobia.[10]

The study "Germany's Muslim Demographic Revolution" by the Gatestone Institute International Policy Council outlines the demographic tsunami sweeping across the Continent. The report quotes a European commissioner who warns: "There are 20 million refugees waiting at the doorstep of Europe."[11] The influx is kindling the fervor of the Muslim community, with mosque attendance doubling in just one month.

More than seven thousand of Germany's Muslim migrants are Salafists—an extreme branch of Islam that is passionately committed to sharia law and vehemently opposed to Germany's democratic order. These radical Muslims are permitted openly to advance their extreme version of Islam.[12] German federal police chief Hans-Georg Maassen claims: "ISIS extremists hardened on the battlefields of Iraq and Syria are blending in with the migrants and are planning 'combat missions' in Europe."[13] His office has identified almost eight thousand Islamic radicals currently in Germany.

By late 2015 there was yet another ominous development as reports surfaced warning that tens of thousands of undocumented refugees are slipping away from holding centers and refugee shelters across Germany. According to *Die Welt,* in the northeastern province of Brandenburg alone nearly half of the migrants have disappeared.[14] Those sneaking out of the centers are described as "completely undocumented" refugees who come from regions of the world that "breed terrorism and violence," and who do not speak German or understand

European culture and mannerisms.[15] The German government is left completely in the dark as to their intentions.

Terror in Paris and San Bernardino

The concerns of the intelligence community were realized in full force on November 13, 2015, when Paris suffered its greatest terror attack in the history of the république. Teams of armed men wearing suicide vests struck at a half-dozen sites in central Paris, roaming at will, firing automatic weapons, killing 130 and wounding hundreds of Parisians and tourists.

The packed audience at the Jewish-owned Bataclan music hall heard what some took initially to be a fireworks display by the U.S. rock group Eagles of Death Metal, which was onstage. Panic broke out as armed gunmen shouting "Allahu Akbar" began shooting indiscriminately into the crowd, as described by one witness: "They didn't stop firing. There was blood everywhere, corpses everywhere. We heard screaming. Everyone was trying to flee."[16] More than eighty were killed before the assailants blew themselves up as French police entered the concert hall.

ISIS was quick to release a statement claiming responsibility, stating that the attack was in retaliation for French military operations against ISIS in Syria. The attack came days after ISIS took credit for suicide bombings that killed dozens in Beirut, Lebanon.

French police were alarmed to discover the multinational composition of the attackers: Syrian and Egyptian passports were found on the bodies of some of the terrorists; others were identified as French nationals of foreign descent. Yet another discovery served to confirm reports that ISIS terrorists were hiding among the masses flooding into Europe: Three of the attackers were carrying Syrian passports and had passed through the Greek island of Leros the previous month.[17]

The implications stunned terrorism experts: ISIS fighters had managed to pass through border controls and gain admission through the continent's porous southern frontier. Those same individuals were able to move unhindered across Europe to France, where they were provided with automatic weapons and suicide vests. They then participated in a highly coordinated and deadly terrorist attack in Paris—all within the time span of several weeks. Intelligence officials had warned that perhaps two of every hundred migrants were terrorists intending to "take the fight" to Europe.

Some of the terrorists were French citizens, second-generation offspring of migrants from Muslim lands, thus debunking the general assumption that the children of immigrants are more Westernized and less likely to hold extremist views. A study conducted by the British think tank Policy Exchange paints a bleak picture of radicalized young British Muslims.

The study found "disturbing evidence of young Muslims adopting more fundamentalist beliefs on key social and political issues than their parents or grandparents."[18] Forty percent of the younger generation of Muslims polled indicated that, far from assimilating to Western culture, they would welcome the institution of sharia law in Britain, even though Islamic law stipulates lashings with a whip, stoning or beheading as punishments for serious crimes. By contrast, only 17 percent of Muslims over age 55 approved of sharia punishments.

After the Paris attack, the obvious question on everyone's mind was, How many others are preparing to commit similar violent attacks? A visibly shaken French President François Hollande denounced the attacks as "a horror" and vowed to wage a "merciless" fight against terrorism. But given the very nature of such acts, where the perpetrators avoid confronting armed police but instead strike "soft" targets, i.e., defenseless civilians, it takes only a very few determined attackers to sow bedlam.

In addition to terrorists secreting themselves among refugees and migrants coming into Europe, an estimated six thousand European Muslims have left for the Middle East to fight with ISIS. Some fifteen hundred are known to have returned, traveling freely on their national passports. The intelligence agencies of their native countries are aware of their activities, but lack the manpower to provide surveillance of every potential security risk. How many of these seasoned fighters are as we speak joining sleeper cells preparing to carry out terrorist attacks?

Many Americans breathed a sigh of relief that ISIS was a European problem that would not directly affect them. Already in July 2015 FBI director James Comey had informed the Aspen Security Forum that ISIS is actively recruiting in all fifty states and "has influenced a significant but unknown number of Americans through a year-long campaign on social media urging Muslims who can't travel to the Middle East to 'kill where you are.'"[19] He noted that Twitter handles affiliated with ISIS have more than 21,000 English-language followers worldwide, including thousands who may be U.S. residents.

It was no idle threat: Since 9/11 dozens of people in the U.S. had been killed in acts of terrorism perpetrated by those claiming to strike in the name of Islamic jihad. In addition, the FBI and law enforcement agencies have thwarted many more Islamist-inspired terrorist plots against Americans, not including failed attempts such as the botched 2010 car bombing of Times Square carried out by a Pakistani-American who received instruction at a terrorist training camp in Pakistan.

On December 2, 2015, the ISIS threat to the United States became reality when Syed Rizwan Farook and Tashfeen Malik, a married couple of Pakistani descent, shot and killed 14 co-workers and seriously injured 22 in a terrorist attack at an office party in San Bernardino, California. The couple were later gunned down by police after a car chase.

Farook and Malik, according to FBI director Comey, had become radicalized abroad: "We also believe they were inspired by foreign terrorist organizations."[20]

In a Facebook post after the shootings, Tashfeen Malik pledged her allegiance to Abu Bakr al-Baghdadi, the emir of the self-proclaimed Islamic State. ISIS exulted in the worst terrorist attack on U.S. soil since September 11, 2001, hailing the couple as supporters of the terror group.

Awakening from a Long Slumber?

Meanwhile in Europe, the increasingly chaotic state of affairs contradicts the narrative of the West's political elite, who remain committed to an open door policy. Eastern Europe takes a more cautious view, having borne the brunt of Muslim invasions through the centuries. Between the eighth and seventeenth centuries the continent fought ten major wars and dozens of regional conflicts against invading Islamic armies.

Viktor Orbán, Prime Minister of Hungary, was roundly criticized by his Western European counterparts for appealing to the continent's noble heritage as he defended the fence that his country erected post haste to stem the raging flood of migrants. The fence was vital, he stated,

> to keep Europe Christian. Those arriving have been raised in another religion, and represent a radically different culture. Most of them are not Christians, but Muslims. This is an important question, because Europe and European identity is rooted in Christianity.[21]

The appeal to the continent's Christian roots resonated among some in the "belly of the beast" of Europe's entrenched secular humanism. In solidarity, Italy's foreign minister stated that the deepening immigration crisis threatened to "rip the soul" out of the European Union. The secretary general of the Danish Refugee Council joined in, warning that the crisis would lead to a total collapse of European society.[22]

While many, including Christians, approve of an ordered migrant policy, the unmanageable flood pouring into Europe has led to a surge of support for political parties that call for stricter immigration policies. Once small and marginalized, the anti-immigration parties in Sweden and Denmark began rising in the polls. The Swiss People's Party won the biggest share in the 2015 national parliamentary elections on a platform of limiting immigration. Also that year in Poland, the anti-immigration Conservative Law and Justice Party swept into power, winning 242 of 460 seats in parliament.

At this writing, in Germany the PEGIDA—or Patriotic Europeans Against the Islamization of the West—movement has been making steady gains as Chancellor Angela Merkel's approval ratings are plummeting. In a bid to outflank PEGIDA's growing popularity, Merkel's own Christian Democratic Union party proposed the construction of Berlin Wall–style defenses on Germany's borders.

France's National Front has rocketed to becoming the country's largest political party. Leader Marine Le Pen compared the surge in migrants coming into Europe to the invasion of Rome by Visigoths:

> Without any action, this migratory influx will be like the barbarian invasion of the fourth century, and the consequences will be the same. . . . We must immediately stop this madness to safeguard our social pact, freedom and identity.[23]

103

Churchill's Insight

In *The River War* a young Winston Churchill recounted his experiences as a British Army officer during the Mahdist War in the Sudan. He recognized that individual Muslims may show admirable qualities, but they are often constrained by a harsh and unyielding religion and culture:

> How dreadful are the curses which Mohammedanism lays on its votaries! Besides the fanatical frenzy, which is as dangerous in a man as hydrophobia in a dog, there is this fearful fatalistic apathy. The effects are apparent in many countries, improvident habits, slovenly systems of agriculture, sluggish methods of commerce, and insecurity of property exist wherever the followers of the Prophet rule or live.
>
> A degraded sensualism deprives this life of its grace and refinement, the next of its dignity and sanctity. The fact that in Mohammedan law every woman must belong to some man as his absolute property, either as a child, a wife, or a concubine, must delay the final extinction of slavery until the faith of Islam has ceased to be a great power among men.
>
> Individual Muslims may show splendid qualities, but the influence of the religion paralyses the social development of those who follow it. No stronger retrograde force exists in the world. Far from being moribund, Mohammedanism is a militant and proselytizing faith. It has already spread throughout Central Africa, raising fearless warriors at every step; and were it not that Christianity is sheltered in the strong arms of science, the science against which it had vainly struggled, the civilization of modern Europe might fall, as fell the civilization of ancient Rome.[24]

Churchill's words may yet prove prophetic, that if not for Christianity, "the civilization of modern Europe might fall." There is yet hope that the continent will find a way to balance the commendable impulse of humanitarianism with its very real security and economic concerns.

We return to the Middle East, whose devastated lands were responsible for driving millions to Europe and beyond. The discovery of massive energy reserves threatens to further de-stabilize the region as nations compete for control of these vital resources, a peril compounded by the fact that these new natural gas fields are located in proximity to the *bête noire* of the Middle East—the despised Jewish State of Israel.

8

Have You Come
to Take Great Plunder?

An old Yiddish joke laments the ill fortune of the Jews, who wandered for forty years before finally settling in the one place in the Middle East that had not a drop of oil. Since its inception, the State of Israel has been almost completely dependent upon foreign sources for its energy needs. As the Jewish state has grown into an impressive industrialized society—with all of the energy-demanding accoutrements of the modern world—its vulnerability to an oil and gas blockade instigated by its enemies has increased accordingly.

That ominous scenario has already occurred. As we have seen, in June 1967 then-Egyptian President Gamal Abdel Nasser ordered the blockade of the Gulf of Aqaba, through which 90 percent of Israel's oil passed. Closing the gulf to Israeli shipping effectively meant the strangling of Israel's economy. It proved to be the final provocation that triggered the start of the Six-Day War.

The tables are turning. In a most remarkable transformation, Israel is moving from energy dependence to becoming a net exporter of fossil fuels. Many believe that this is in fulfillment of a cryptic reference to Gog and Magog invading Israel "to seize much plunder." Could this be a reference to Israel's newly acquired oil and gas wealth, a valuable commodity that is coveted by her energy-poor enemies?

Well-heeled investors including media magnate Rupert Murdoch and banker Lord Jacob Rothschild have invested heavily in the quest for oil in Israel. Over the past several decades more than four hundred wells have been drilled at various locations across Israel, sometimes using clues from the Bible—with few to none turning up commercial quantities of oil and gas.

Asher Shall Dip His Foot in Oil

World War II fighter pilot and petroleum engineer Andy SoRelle raised millions of dollars for his efforts to drill for oil on the Mediterranean coast in the north of Israel. He believed that a prophecy about Asher, the grandson of Noah, referred to petroleum wealth: "Most blessed of sons is Asher; let him be favored by his brothers, and let him bathe his feet in oil" (Deuteronomy 33:24).

The land of Canaan was divided among the twelve tribes of Israel. SoRelle checked maps of Israel in biblical times for the territory of Asher, which indeed bore a resemblance to a leg. He became convinced that the "toe" of Asher's territory was located at the Roman port of Caesarea along the shores of the Mediterranean Sea.

SoRelle made the common mistake of interpreting the biblical text in the light of modern understanding instead of the historical period and culture in which it was written. *Oil* in

Scripture refers to olive oil, an important commodity that was a basic foodstuff as well as an ingredient in perfume, medicine, etc. Petroleum was not known in the biblical world, nor would the people of that day have had any use for it. Viewed in its historic context, the promise to Asher was that of an abundance of olive oil, i.e., financial blessing.

Based upon his interpretation of the "toe" of Asher, in 1982 SoRelle began drilling at Caesarea. After two years of effort he managed to bore down to 21,500 feet and found traces of petroleum. The news electrified Christians in the U.S.: "Across the Bible Belt, the faithful braced for a gusher. On *The 700 Club*, Pat Robertson reported that [SoRelle] was about to tap 'the largest oil field ever discovered,' a development that could 'revolutionize the fulfillment of biblical prophecy.'"[1] SoRelle's plans, however, came to naught when the drilling equipment jammed, making further operations impossible.

After decades of fruitless searching at various locations around the country, at long last black gold was discovered. The Israeli subsidiary of the U.S. company Genie Energy began exploratory drilling on the Golan Heights, the territory east of the Sea of Galilee that was captured from Syria in the Six-Day War. In 2015 what promised to be an enormous oil and natural gas reserve was discovered in rock strata that is more than ten times thicker than the average strata worldwide, indicating tremendous potential. The chief geologist of the Israeli drilling company estimated that the reservoir had the "potential of billions of barrels."[2]

Development of the new field, however, will be fraught with danger as it lies in close proximity to the Syrian border. Literally only a few miles away ISIS and other jihadi groups are battling the Syrian army and its Lebanon-based Hezbollah proxy force. In addition to being at each other's throats, these warring factions are also the sworn enemies of Israel.

Israel has annexed the Golan Heights, although the U.S. and most of the international community do not recognize its claims to sovereignty. Damascus insists that the Golan belongs to Syria despite the fact that it lost the territory in a war of aggression against Israel. Israel has refused to give over the territory as it has been used repeatedly as a staging ground for attacks on Israel and for raining mortars and shells down upon Galilean towns and kibbutzim (communal settlements).

Air raid sirens across the Golan Heights sound the warning periodically as mortar shells and rockets are fired from Syria. Defending oil and gas fields with their highly flammable infrastructure and pipelines, etc., from enemy fire would be a daunting challenge. If the Israelis are able to develop successfully what some observers are calling an underground oil shale reserve that rivals that of Saudi Arabia, it will fundamentally change the geopolitical and economic balance of the Middle East. In that scenario, protecting such a prized resource from the enemies of the Jewish state will become a national imperative.

Leviathan

When it rains it pours. Deep within the waters of the Mediterranean Sea immense energy depositories have recently been discovered that, one headline predicts, "could completely change the world as we know it."[3] In 2010, U.S. Noble Energy and its Israeli partners discovered a natural gas field within Israel's territorial waters in the Mediterranean. The field contains an estimated 600 billion cubic meters, double the gas reserves of the United Kingdom. The hydrocarbons from the aptly named Leviathan field are sufficient to meet Israel's needs, saving the country more than $130 billion in energy costs as well as constituting a potential source of exports to Europe and Asia.

Leviathan is not the only colossal gas field discovered off the coast of Israel. To the southeast lies the Tamar reservoir, which contains an estimated 280 billion cubic meters of gas. Nearby Tamar Southwest reservoir adds some 19 billion cubic meters, with more to come as drilling activity intensifies. These massive gas fields are expected to meet Israel's domestic needs for decades to come, with surplus gas from Leviathan slated to be used for export.

And that is just the beginning. According to the U.S. Geological Survey, Leviathan could hold more than 600 million barrels of recoverable oil—enough to satisfy Israel's consumption for years to come.

The eastern Mediterranean is proving to hold a treasure trove of natural gas and oil deposits. In 2015 an Italian company discovered a gas field off the coast of Egypt that eclipses Leviathan. The as yet undeveloped Zohr field is estimated at 850 billion cubic meters, the equivalent of 5.5 billion barrels of oil. Production will require very expensive drilling at 1,450 meters below sea level, but could be the best economic news that Egypt has received in years, allowing for energy self-sufficiency and industrial growth.

Added to the mix is Israel's northern neighbor, Lebanon, where fields have been discovered that could hold as much as 2 billion cubic meters of gas reserves and 865 million barrels of oil. While together these recent finds pale in comparison to the vast oil and gas fields in Saudi Arabia, the Gulf States and Iran, they have unique economic value because of their strategic location.

Exclusive Economic Zones

According to international law, an Exclusive Economic Zone (EEZ) generally extends two hundred miles from the coast.

But coastlines are rarely straight, causing overlapping of the respective lines drawn by neighboring countries. The United Nations Convention on the Law of the Sea stipulates that countries are expected to work out the boundaries, with contested underwater natural gas or oil fields belonging to the nearest country.

Problems arise when the countries are adversaries, as has historically been the case in the eastern Mediterranean. Lebanon, for example, refused to negotiate an EEZ with Israel, which then drew its own lines in conjunction with Cyprus. After Israel discovered natural gas in its sector, Lebanon submitted an EEZ to the U.N. that included the Israeli gas fields, setting the stage for future conflict between the two countries.

Egypt's Zohr field could become another point of contention. The full extent of the deposits is still not known and could well extend into disputed territory with Israel. Likewise, Egypt could infringe upon or claim ownership of Israeli fields close to Israel's southern maritime border.

The locations of these recently discovered fields in proximity to thirsty importers of oil such as Europe and Turkey magnify their importance—and could make Israel a prime target for jihadist groups or nations opposed to the Jewish state. Ungainly drilling rigs towering hundreds of feet above the sea would be sitting ducks for standoff weapons—as in 1988, when during the U.S.-led Operation Praying Mantis coalition air and surface units destroyed Iranian oil rigs in the Persian Gulf.

In addition, a successful attack upon the single existing pipeline running ninety miles underwater from Leviathan to the receiving terminal in Ashdod would disrupt 70 percent of Israel's power supply. Recognizing the vulnerability, Israel is racing to complete additional underwater pipelines to safeguard the transport of gas from the Tamar and Leviathan fields.

Flashpoint Gaza

Fighting for control of offshore gas fields claimed by both Israel and the Palestinian Authority could well ignite a regional conflict and become a pretext for commencing hostilities against the Jewish state. Extensive gas reserves off the coastline of Gaza have been reported by British Gas, working under an agreement signed with the PA. The agreement authorized the development of offshore gas facilities and the construction of a gas pipeline.

In 2000 British Gas drilled two wells and estimated the reserves to be of the order of 400 billion cubic meters—a discovery on a par with some of the larger Israeli fields. The Gaza Marine gas field was expected to make the Palestinian territories energy sufficient, with a surplus left over for export.

Initially the project was presented as an opportunity for co-operation between Israel and the Palestinian state, with benefits for both parties. The political atmosphere in Gaza became radicalized, however, when Hamas took de facto control in 2007, and it soon became clear that partnership on any level with Israel was impossible.

That perception has been confirmed by the ongoing Gaza-Israeli conflict, which has erupted in a series of intense conflagrations since 2004. At last count following Israel's withdrawal from the Gaza Strip in 2005, Hamas has fired more than 11,000 rockets into the country, an average of more than three attacks every day, leaving hundreds of thousands of Israelis living in fear. The rockets are capable of reaching Israel's most populous metropolitan areas: Tel Aviv and Jerusalem.

The terrorists' arsenal includes the formidable M-302, with a warhead of 144 kilograms and a range of one hundred miles. The weapons that Hamas is using against Israel are being supplied by Iran, properly called a rogue state because of its blatant disregard for international law and convention by intervening to attack and overthrow neighboring states.

The presence of contested oil and natural gas fields in a region that is experiencing such high volatility could serve as an inducement for energy-poor nations to secure their access to those reserves. One nation that is highly dependent upon energy imports has been demonstrating increasing hostility toward Israel—and it has a historic connection with Gog and Magog.

A *Casus Belli*

Relations between Turkey and Israel have deteriorated as we have seen—after decades of friendly cooperation across a number of spheres, including trade, tourism and military. In 1949 the Turkish republic was the first Muslim country to recognize the State of Israel. Since the election of Recep Erdoğan to the position of prime minister in 2003, however, relations have become increasingly strained.

Erdoğan has been outspoken against Israeli occupation and settlement activity on the West Bank, and heads one of the few nations admitting to providing material support to Hamas. Relations between Ankara and Jerusalem reached a new low in 2010 when Israel intercepted and boarded the *Mavi Marmara*, the flagship of the flotilla that sailed from Turkey to Gaza and attempted to enter what Israel considered its territorial waters— the very waters where immense gas fields have been discovered.

Israeli commandos boarded the six ships, and during the ensuing fight ten Turkish activists were killed. Turkey suspended defense industry ties with Israel and downgraded diplomatic relations. Ambassadors were withdrawn from Tel Aviv and Ankara.

Despite the worsening relations, the two nations share a common interest that one day could potentially lead to conflict: energy. Israel assumed initially that it had a ready customer in Egypt for its vast offshore Tamar and Leviathan gas fields.

That was before the discovery of the enormous Zohr field that is expected to meet Egypt's natural gas needs for the foreseeable future.

Turkey, on the other hand, finds itself in the unenviable position of experiencing rapid growth while lacking domestic energy sources to fuel its expanding economy. Turkey imports 91 percent of its oil and 99 percent of its natural gas, making Israel's newfound discoveries a potential source of energy. The two countries have been negotiating an undersea pipeline linking the Tamar and Leviathan. In the words of one Turkish energy expert:

> Demand for gas in Turkey is rising at the fastest rate in the world, and Turkey is looking to diversify sources of supply and reduce its dependence on Russian gas. Israeli gas that reaches Turkey can also be exported to Europe. A deal between Israel and Turkey is a win-win situation for the two countries.[4]

It could also trigger Armageddon. Should the undersea pipeline be built, it would lead to a Muslim country being dependent upon the Jewish state for a vital energy source. If at some point in the future the political winds change from cool to frigid, one can imagine Turkey taking action under the pretext of safeguarding its access to natural gas.

Given the trend toward extremism under Erdoğan, the humiliation of having to rely upon Jews for an important commodity could also trigger military aggression. A 2014 Pew Research Center poll found that out of nine countries surveyed, Turkish citizens had the least favorable opinion of Israel, with only 2 percent holding a favorable view.[5]

With the world's eighth largest military force and a navy of some two hundred active ships, the historic land of Gog and Magog is fully capable of mounting a potent offensive in Israel's direction. If Turkey joins with Muslim allies in central

Asia, Iran and North Africa, one can visualize the makings of a military juggernaut of biblical proportions that will one day be directed against Israel.

But first the world must hear hoofbeats once more out of the book of Revelation: "Then another horse came out, a fiery red one. Its rider was given power to take peace from the earth and to make people kill each other. To him was given a large sword" (6:4).

We will now examine a prophetic scenario whereby Christendom stands on the brink of a decision of monumental importance. Will the United States and Europe recover their spiritual heritage and attendant vitality so that they can rise to challenge Gog and Magog? Or, enfeebled, will these former bastions of Christianity be overrun like Rome of old?

PART 3

TWILIGHT
OF THE WEST

9

Beyond the Pillars of Hercules

Sheba and Dedan and the merchants of Tarshish
and all her villages will say to you, "Have you come
to plunder? Have you gathered your hordes to loot,
to carry off silver and gold, to take away livestock
and goods and to seize much plunder?"

Ezekiel 38:13

A reappraisal of the historical evidence sheds new light on this
cryptic reference in Ezekiel's prophecy regarding the challenge
directed at Gog and Magog, and may point to a role in end
time prophecy for the United States. The puzzling wording
of those speaking seems to indicate a nation with a stake in
the region, but it is unclear whether the verse indicates determined resolve—or an erstwhile great power that is no longer
capable of defending her borders, as in a morally emasculated
America.

The first two entities in this passage, Sheba and Dedan, are readily identified as a nomadic people who wandered through the desert wastes of Arabia. We first read of them in the book of Genesis, where they are identified as descendants of Abraham through his concubine Keturah:

> Abraham had taken another wife, whose name was Keturah. She bore him Zimran, Jokshan, Medan, Midian, Ishbak and Shuah. Jokshan was the father of Sheba and Dedan; the descendants of Dedan were the Ashurites, the Letushites and the Leummites. The sons of Midian were Ephah, Epher, Hanok, Abida and Eldaah. All these were descendants of Keturah. Abraham left everything he owned to Isaac. But while he was still living, he gave gifts to the sons of his concubines and sent them away from his son Isaac to the land of the east.
>
> Genesis 25:1–6

The "land of the east" is the deserts of Arabia. Greek historian and geographer Ptolemy mentions that Zimran founded the region of Zabram west of Mecca.[1] The descendants of his brother Jokshan have also been associated with tribes in Arabia Felix on the eastern side of the Arabian Peninsula.

This vast trackless territory ranges from the Red Sea in the west to Persia and Assyria. The few hardy inhabitants lived a nomadic life, pitching their goat hair tents and depending upon the "ships of the desert" to provide milk for sustenance and transport from oasis to oasis. Until the nineteenth century these Bedouin had little to offer the outside world by way of trade except coffee beans, dates and spices.

That all changed in the twentieth century when oil was discovered, first in Iran in 1908 and then in Arabia in the 1930s. The timing could not have been more advantageous since, as I mentioned earlier, the British Empire, the preeminent maritime power of the day, was retrofitting its vast fleets to run on oil rather than coal. Virtually overnight the Arabian sheiks were catapulted from a marginal existence to possessing unheard of wealth, with much more to come.

The desert nomads possessed few weapons with which to protect themselves and their burgeoning wealth, and quickly became dependent upon the Western powers for their security. The fears of vulnerable Sheba and Dedan about invaders coming "to seize much plunder" would not have made sense until the last century. As we have seen, recent discoveries of undersea natural gas fields in the eastern Mediterranean serve to further heighten the attraction of the Middle East to energy-poor predatory nations.

The merchants of Tarshish is thought to refer to Tartessos (Tartessus), the ancient name of a city-state near the mouth of the Guadalquivir River on the southwest coast of Andalusia.[2] The former Phoenician settlement of Joppa traded with Tartessos, hence the biblical prophet Jonah's attempt to flee to that remote destination. Herodotus describes these seafaring people as residing beyond the Pillars of Hercules—known today as the Strait of Gibraltar.[3]

The Romans called the principal port of Tartessos "Gades," which by the twelfth century was morphed into Cádiz—the oldest continuously inhabited city in Spain and one of the oldest in Europe. The city has been a principal homeport of the Spanish Navy since the eighteenth century. Even earlier the city experienced a renaissance during the Age of Exploration in the fifteenth to eighteenth centuries.

This latter fact is of particular note for our investigations as this stretch of the Andalusian coastline was to play a central role in the conquest of the Americas. It was from Cádiz and nearby ports in the region of Tartessos—biblical Tarshish—that Christopher Columbus set sail for the New World.

Cádiz became the home port of the Spanish treasure fleet and was instrumental in the settlement and Christianization of the New World. It was admittedly a checkered history, with the efforts of the Roman Catholic Church often connected—rightly or wrongly—with the rapacious quest for treasure on the part of the *conquistadores*. Yet it is also undeniable that it was Franciscan missionaries hailing from the southwestern coast of Spain who led the way—often at great cost—in introducing the native peoples of the Americas to the Christian faith.

The "villages" of Tarshish, a major seafaring power, are believed to refer to her colonies in far-flung places. The descendants of the inhabitants of the region of Tarshish along the Andalusian coast in Spain—in the person of Christopher Columbus and those following after him—established colonies in the New World that eventually became the Americas.

An alternate reading of the text in Ezekiel has "Tarshish, with all the young lions thereof" (Ezekiel 38:13 KJV). The lion is the national emblem of Great Britain. Some have suggested that "young lions" refers to the British colonies, which include the United States. Support for this view is found in another verse in Ezekiel: "Tarshish did business with you because of your great wealth of goods; they exchanged silver, iron, tin and lead for your merchandise" (27:12).

The key word here is *tin*—a valuable metal used in the making of bronze, the discovery of which revolutionized ancient warfare, as bronze is much stronger than copper. King Solomon used "great quantities of bronze" (2 Chronicles 4:18 NLT) in the building of the Temple and for outfitting his soldiers.

There were few sources of tin in the biblical world: A major supplier from 2000 BC was Brittany and Cornwall in England. The verse in Ezekiel suggests that ships of Tarshish brought tin from what would one day become Great Britain, known as the "lion."

Thus the United States is indicated in the Ezekiel text as one of the powers that challenge Gog and Magog. Still to be determined is whether America rises from a position of strength or is unable to muster more than a feeble protest. But first we must examine another mystical text in Revelation.

Mystery Babylon

Students of biblical prophecy have long sought to identify an enigmatic world power that comes to a sudden and catastrophic end at the end of days—a calamity so auspicious that it occupies a full two chapters of the book of Revelation.

> The name written on her forehead was a mystery:
> BABYLON THE GREAT
> THE MOTHER OF PROSTITUTES
> AND OF THE ABOMINATIONS OF THE EARTH.
>
> Revelation 17:5

As we shall see, the destruction of this major world power, named here as Mystery Babylon, removes a major obstacle to the designs of Gog and Magog. Some Protestant prophecy teachers believe that Revelation is speaking about a religious power and argue that Mystery Babylon is none other than Rome and the Vatican. Some point to the likelihood that a political power, the United States, fills the requirements. And some consider it to be Istanbul. Let's look briefly at the likelihood of these three candidates.

The Vatican: The City on Seven Hills

The proponents of the view that the Roman Catholic Church is Mystery Babylon begin by pointing to Revelation 17:9: "This calls for a mind with wisdom. The seven heads are seven hills on which the woman sits." The text indeed appears to refer to Rome, for according to tradition Romulus founded the

original city on the Palatine Hill, which was at the time surrounded by six other small settlements that eventually merged
into one city.

And in fact *Babylon* is a code word for *Rome* in extra-biblical
works such as the Sibylline Oracles (5, 159f.), the Apocalypse of
Baruch (ii, 1) and the Jewish Apocalypse of Ezra (3:1). In the
New Testament, Saint Peter is believed to have been in Rome
when he wrote, "The church that is at Babylon . . . saluteth
you" (1 Peter 5:13 KJV).

According to the late Protestant apologist Dave Hunt, the
Roman Catholic Church is a preeminent worldly economic
power with an unholy goal: "Her popes have built an unrivaled
worldwide empire of property, wealth, and influence. . . . The
Church today still ceaselessly seeks to bring under its control
all mankind and all their goods."[4]

There are, to be sure, curious similarities between the description of the Great Harlot of Mystery Babylon and some
of the traditions of the Roman Catholic Church. Revelation
17:4 tells us that the Great Harlot is "dressed in purple and
scarlet." Some pointed out similarities with the priestly cas-
sock: "The close-fitting, ankle-length robe worn by the Catholic clergy as their official garb. . . . The color for bishops and
other prelates is purple, for cardinals scarlet. . . ."[5] Yet these
royal colors have also been worn by innumerable potentates
throughout history.

Claims that the the Roman Catholic Church is by far the
wealthiest institution on earth and thus fits the description of
fantastically wealthy Mystery Babylon must also be qualified.
If one hangs on the word *institution*, then any institution
with a billion members with all the attendant buildings and
property would necessarily possess considerable wealth. Critics of the church make much of its alleged "fabulous wealth"
in the form of art treasures and documents in the Vatican

museum and elsewhere. But these are not assets intended to be sold any more than if a museum were to put price tags on its artifacts.

Some point to the "golden cup" (chalice) in the hand (Revelation 17:4) of the "great harlot" (verse 1 NASB) as identifying the Roman Catholic Church: "[It is] the most important of the sacred vessels. . . . [It] may be of gold or silver, and if the latter, then the inside must be surfaced with gold."[6] While true that thousands of such chalices are kept in Catholic churches around the world, golden cups have since time immemorial been associated with royalty, the wealthy and conquerors. As we have seen, the Ottoman Sultan Suleiman was renowned for drinking from solid gold vessels.

Also questionable are attempts to identify the Roman Catholic Church with the Great Harlot on the grounds that, like that wicked personage, the church has supposedly practiced evil to gather her wealth, filling the golden chalice with "abominations and filthiness" (Revelation 17:4 KJV). Surely there is a long list of candidates in the history of mankind that have been responsible for such reprehensible evil.

The Spanish Inquisition is commonly brought up as a prime example of injustices committed by Christians—in particular the Roman Catholic Church. This is based largely upon wildly exaggerated claims made in outdated nineteenth-century works. R. W. Thompson, writing in 1876, states that "in Spain alone the number of condemned exceeded 3 million, with about 300,000 burned at the stake."[7]

More recent scholarship has corrected this misleading picture. In *The Spanish Inquisition: A Historical Revision*, renowned historian Henry Kamen states: "We can in all probability accept the estimate, made on the basis of available documentation, that a maximum of three thousand persons may have suffered death during the entire history of the tribunal."[8] This measured judgment is echoed by another prominent historian, Edward Peters, who concludes:

> [T]he Spanish Inquisition, in spite of wildly inflated estimates of the numbers of its victims, acted with considerable restraint in inflicting the death penalty, far more restraint than was demonstrated in secular tribunals elsewhere in Europe that dealt with the same kinds of offenses. The best estimate is that around 3000 death sentences were carried out in Spain by Inquisitorial verdict between 1550 and 1800, a far smaller number than that in comparable secular courts.[9]

While the unjust killing of even a single individual is in no wise justifiable, it beggars logic to claim that among the sordid compendium of the world's atrocities, the Inquisition is the fulfillment of the "abominations and filthiness" committed by the Great Harlot of Revelation.

There is one final incongruity with identifying the Roman Catholic Church as the Great Harlot of Revelation who sits "on seven hills." While Rome is indeed built upon seven hills that are within the original walls of the city on the east bank of the Tiber, the Vatican hill is not among them. The seat of the Roman Catholic Church is west of the Tiber, outside the walls, and was not incorporated into the city of Rome until the ninth century AD. Thus the area was not part of the Rome of "seven hills" that the New Testament writers knew.

The United States

A number of American commentators, ironically, are convinced that Mystery Babylon, the Great Harlot of Revelation 17–18, is a reference to none other than the United States. They find it improbable that there should be no reference in the eschatological texts to what is arguably the wealthiest and most powerful nation in the history of the world.

The description of Mystery Babylon in Revelation 18 does appear to lend support to identification with the United States. We read that "the merchants of the earth grew rich from her excessive luxuries" (18:3). And again: "The merchants of the earth will weep and mourn over her because no one buys their cargoes anymore" (18:11).

This is an apt description of the trade relationship between a wealthy United States, the economic engine of the modern world, and her trading partners. The United States holds the world's largest economy, accounting for more than 20 percent of the global domestic product. The U.S. dollar is the world's foremost reserve currency and the preeminent legal tender used in international transactions.

The financial health of more than a few nations depends upon their ability to market their goods to American consumers. Whereas many countries block imports to protect their economies, the free trade policy of the United States has made it the premier destination of much of the world's products, and has resulted in trade deficits with many nations. The sudden loss of such a preeminent market would indeed cause great consternation around the world.

This theme is echoed in Revelation 18:7: "Give her as much torment and grief as the glory and luxury she gave herself." Undeniably, the United States has provided a standard of living for its citizens that is the envy of the rest of the world. Although many Americans do not consider their lifestyles to be "luxurious," the fact is that much of the world exists in appallingly substandard conditions, lacking basic necessities such as decent housing, electricity and potable water. For them the United States is the unattainable dream.

The text continues: "In her heart she boasts, 'I sit enthroned as queen. I am not a widow; I will never mourn'" (Revelation 18:7). This is taken to refer to the fact that the United States has never been defeated in time of war against foreign enemies, a boast that few other nations can make. American military might—though steadily diminishing—is respected and feared around the globe.

One important aspect of the Great Harlot, however, is difficult to identify with the United States. It is by no means certain that the U.S. stands out among the nations as being guilty of perpetrating the "abominations and filthiness" of the Great Harlot. We also read that "the woman was drunk with the blood of God's holy people, the blood of those who bore testimony to Jesus" (Revelation 17:6). Whatever the shortcomings of the United States, few would argue that America is responsible for the martyrdom of Christians on a mass scale.

As we shall presently see, it is well within the realm of possibility that the United States could reject its Judeo-Christian heritage and embark upon the wholesale persecution of Christians. First, however, let's look at one other possible identification of the Great Harlot that historically corresponds to the biblical description.

Istanbul

Few may be aware that another Mediterranean city with an illustrious—and checkered—history is said to be built on seven hills: the great Turkish city of Istanbul—formerly Constantinople. The Emperor Constantine modeled the former Byzantine capital after Rome's seven hills. Istanbul also fits another description of the Great Harlot, who "sits by many waters" (Revelation 17:1). Unlike Rome, which is located well inland, Istanbul "sits" near numerous bodies of water, including the

Sea of Marmara, the Bosporus Strait, the Black Sea, the Aegean Sea, the Sea of Crete and the Mediterranean Sea.

In addition, Istanbul uniquely fulfills the description of the Great Harlot as a great persecutor of Christians. The fall of Constantinople in 1453 was one of the seminal turning points of European history. More than half a millennium later there are striking parallels between the historical accounts of the murderous violence perpetrated by the Muslim invaders of Constantinople and the barbaric acts of the Islamic state and other jihadi groups in our time—a continuity rooted in the Muslim fixation with jihad against Christians, Jews and other "nonbelievers."

When the Ottoman Turks broke through the walls, "the unhappy city was abandoned to unspeakable excesses of cruelty and debauchery."[10] Untold thousands perished by the sword: They were the lucky ones. Those who survived were subjected to rape and the plundering of their homes and possessions. More than half of the population was sold into slavery, flooding the Turkish human chattel markets with cheap captives. For his pleasure, the Turkish commander Mahomet had leading citizens and officials arrested and beheaded in his presence.

The parallels with the Muslim fanaticism of our day are palpable. The world has been subjected to gruesome decapitation videos of Christians and others, which has become the hallmark of radical Islam, bringing to mind this verse in Revelation:

> And I saw the souls of those who had been beheaded because of their testimony about Jesus and because of the word of God. They had not worshiped the beast or its image and had not received its mark on their foreheads or their hands.
>
> Revelation 20:4

From the fall of Constantinople to the Siege of Vienna (1453–1683), the Ottoman Empire was guilty of the slaughter of untold numbers of Christians as it sought to conquer Europe over a period of two hundred years.

After another two centuries of stagnation, the murderous violence against the "unbeliever" resumed during World War I, when between 1914 and 1923 a total of more than 3.5 million Orthodox Greek, Armenian and Assyrian Christians were systematically killed in one final murderous paroxysm as the Ottoman Empire lay in its death throes. The victims were subject to deportation, abduction, torture and massacre. Those who escaped immediate slaughter were driven into the desert to die of thirst and hunger after their homes and villages had been sacked and their wealth expropriated.

In 1948 the United Nations Genocide Convention condemned the Armenian Genocide as a crime against humanity. The present-day Republic of Turkey adamantly denies that the genocide took place, dismissing the charges as mere allegations.

While the city of Istanbul—as emblematic of the Turkish people—certainly fulfills some aspects of the Great Harlot of Revelation, it does not possess the all-surpassing wealth that causes the peoples of the world to lament its destruction.

The Time of the End

When the various candidates have been examined, we come back to one indisputable fact: The results wrought from the destruction of Mystery Babylon demand that it refer to a surpassing economic power that overshadows the world's economy, and whose sudden end brings devastation to the "merchants of the earth."

The truth is, the identity of this power that experiences a great economic downfall and is culpable for the "blood of the saints" is as yet unclear. Perhaps it is best to remember the command of the angel to Daniel concerning his prophecies:

"Seal the words of the scroll until the time of the end" (Daniel 12:4). The interpretation of much of the symbolism found in the book of Revelation will likely only become clear to those who are living at the time of its fulfillment.

We will explore further the implications for identifying the United States as Mystery Babylon, but for now let's turn our attention to the meaning of one cryptic reference in Revelation, one that has puzzled commentators for years: How can it be that Mystery Babylon is said to be destroyed "in one hour" (18:10)?

Perhaps this is not as impossible as it might seem. Let us consider for a moment the world we live in—and for discussion's sake, let's view this as a citizen of the United States. The technological progress that has characterized Western civilization over the past two centuries has provided a standard of living that our forefathers could scarcely dream of. Yet at the same time, life in modern 21st-century America is hopelessly fragile—in many ways resembling the proverbial house of cards that is but one disaster away from total collapse. We will now turn to an examination of just how that unimaginable scenario could become reality.

10

The One-Second War

> "When the kings of the earth who committed adultery with her and shared her luxury see the smoke of her burning, they will weep and mourn over her. Terrified at her torment, they will stand far off and cry: 'Woe! Woe to you, great city, you mighty city of Babylon! In one hour your doom has come!'"
>
> Revelation 18:9–10

Waking up naturally after a full night's rest, you are instantly alarmed by the position of the sun outside your bedroom window. Turning over, you see that your bedside clock is dead. Power outage! Dismayed at being late for work, you catapult out of bed and use the remaining hot water to shower by candlelight.

The first indication that this is something more than a neighborhood power outage comes when you jump into your car and cannot get it to start. Then you notice that several of your neighbors are milling about outside looking confused. No one knows what is happening. Inexplicably, even battery-powered radios are not working.

You do not yet grasp the fact that life as you know it has come to an end, with horrific consequences across the United States.

While you slept, a low-yield nuclear-tipped ballistic missile detonated high in the stratosphere after being launched from a freighter off the East Coast. The explosion triggered a gigantic electromagnetic pulse (EMP) that in a millisecond destroyed the United States' electrical grid, substations and critical infrastructure, along with virtually all electronic components in vehicles, appliances and devices. The prophetic words of a report by the Federal Energy Regulatory Commission have suddenly become reality: "EMP events occur with little or no warning and can have catastrophic effects, including causing outages to major portions of the U.S. power grid possibly lasting for months or longer."[1]

The very technology that created the highest standard of living in the history of the planet has proved to be our undoing. The circuit boards and electronic components that drove virtually everything that we have come to depend upon to sustain our modern way of life—from electric power to telecommunications, transportation and financial transactions—are useless. Municipal water and sewage systems as well as the production, transportation and retailing of food, medicine and other essentials are now shut down.

Pandemonium reigns. With the radio and television silent and all transportation brought to a halt, the terrified populace is left to speculate what happened. As the food in our refrigerators begins to spoil, many make their way to the closest supermarket, which is closed. With computer systems down, retail businesses have no way of processing transactions, even in the unlikely possibility that their employees show up for work. Those grocery stores that improvise cash-only transactions find that their stocks are quickly depleted.

In an instant the nation has been catapulted back into the nineteenth century. And how many will survive? The EMP Commission established by the U.S. Congress in the wake of 9/11 has estimated that within twelve months of a nationwide blackout "up to 90% of the U.S. population could possibly perish from starvation, disease and societal breakdown."[2]

The first victims—dying as you slept that fateful night—were passengers and crews on the hundreds of red-eye flights across the country. With the electronics systems rendered useless, the planes became giant coffins hurtling into the ground.

The sudden destruction of passengers and crews is, perhaps, a dark mercy compared with the rest of us, doomed to suffer a lingering demise beset with unimaginable confusion and panic. Water has ceased flowing from our faucets and our toilets clog, driving us to find a source of potable water. Not having secured a means of water purification in advance, most of us are eventually forced to drink whatever water is available, with the predictable consequences. But there is no use rushing to the nearby hospital, for all medical facilities have ceased operation. Abandoned, their wards have become the stinking depositories of decaying bodies.

Appeals to the police or any government agency are useless. The vast bureaucracy that we have come to depend upon evaporated as civil servants cower at home like the rest of us, frantically wondering how to procure enough food and water to survive. And all in a great void of silence, as telecommunications and public media no longer exist.

One can only imagine the ongoing chaos: Many will suffer in silence, slowly starving and enduring the effects of drinking polluted water as they wait in vain for help to arrive. Others will riot in the streets, breaking into stores in search of food and other necessities. Farms will be plundered by looters escaping the cities to roam the countryside until there is nothing left.

The Grid Goes Down

The electrical grid—the nation's entire network of generation, transmission and distribution—could take years to repair, as many essential components are not manufactured in the United States.

To illustrate this point, let us examine the difficulties with replacing one key component: large power transformers (LPTs), which can weigh hundreds of tons. Only 15 percent of America's LPT demand is met through domestic production. One can assume that in the wake of a devastating nuclear EMP, all domestic LPT producers would instantly shut down due to a lack of electrical power. This leaves foreign producers. The process of building and shipping LPTs to the United States can take up to sixteen months or longer.

Once the foreign-built LPTs arrive on our shores the challenge has only begun, as according to the DOE report there are only about thirty specialized Schnabel cars—monster railcars with twenty axles—in the whole of North America capable of transporting the huge LPTs. Assuming that the oversized railcars can be brought to the point of debarkation, they would then have to maneuver a crippled rail system strewn with broken trains and nonfunctioning switching. And when the first LPT is miraculously delivered to its destination, there are untold others awaiting replacement: The DOE estimates the number of LPTs in the United States to be in the range of tens of thousands.

The Nuclear EMP Naysayers

The widespread concern in intelligence and military circles regarding nuclear EMPs has its detractors, and let us pray that they are correct in assuring us that such an event will not occur.

EMP warfare has been a tried-and-true doomsday weapon for decades—even as far back as the early 1960s—as described by former CIA director and co-chair of the EMP Coalition R. James Woolsey: "For example, in 1961 and 1962, the USSR conducted several EMP tests in Kazakhstan above its own territory, deliberately destroying the electric grid and other critical infrastructures over an area larger than Western Europe."[3]

This was at a time when solid-state electronics and computer chips were still a thing of the future. And as we have seen, modern power grids are more advanced and cover more territory. The effects of these blasts in 1962 were much less than could be expected in the present day. A few properly placed nuclear explosions could have devastating EMP consequences.

Evidence is mounting that rogue nations have the capacity to fit intercontinental missiles with nuclear weapons. In a blockbuster admission Admiral Bill Gortney, commander of North American Aerospace Defense Command (NORAD) and U.S. Northern Command (USNORTHCOM), disclosed that the Pentagon now believes North Korea has mastered the ability to miniaturize its nuclear bombs so they can be fitted onto their latest mobile KN-08 intercontinental ballistic missiles (ICBMs), which are capable of reaching the continental United States.[4]

Those who are quick to dismiss the nuclear EMP threat are at pains to explain why, if no threat exists, the U.S. Congress established the EMP Commission in the wake of the 9/11 terror attacks to determine the "nature and magnitude of potential high-altitude EMP threats to the United States from all potentially hostile states." The Commission determined that within a year of a nationwide power blackout perhaps as few as 10 percent of the U.S. population would still be alive.[5]

They also minimize the fact that the U.S. military appears to be taking the threat very seriously. The North American Aerospace Defense recently approved a $700 million contract to restore the Colorado Cheyenne Mountain facility, which was designed to withstand a nuclear EMP attack. The Air Force moved out of the facility in 2006, but now appears ready to prepare Cheyenne Mountain as a bulwark against just such an attack.

Stranger than Fiction

The novel *One Second After* by William Forstchen caused a stir with its stark portrayal of the effects of an EMP strike. Set in Black Mountain, a small town in North Carolina, the book tells the story of one man's struggle to save his family after nuclear missiles are launched from offshore container ships in the Gulf of Mexico and detonated in the upper atmosphere over the Midwest.

The book describes a rolling sequence of "die offs" as food, clean water and medicine are gone in a matter of weeks, leading to mass starvation and epidemics. With zero communication, no one has any idea what has happened. Mad Max bands roam the countryside plundering what little food, fuel and other supplies have not already been seized by mobs of starving people fleeing the desolate cities. Harvests and stock that remain lie rotting and dying for lack of operating machinery and electricity, and no means to bring them to market.

After one year the U.S. population in *One Second After* had been reduced from 300 million to 30 million. Those with off-the-grid survival skills living in rural areas fared best, with about 50 percent still alive. With their irreplaceable resources quickly depleted and a desperate population reduced to fighting in the streets, metropolitan areas were the hardest hit, with a death rate of 95 percent.

Only after limited communications were restored did the remaining residents learn that an alliance between Iran and North

Korea was responsible for the EMP attack. The survivors also discovered that the United States they knew was no more. The West Coast was under the control of a half-million-strong occupation force from the People's Republic of China, while Mexico had seized control of Texas and the American Southwest.

One Second After contains a nonfiction postscript by U.S. Navy Captain William Sanders, which reminds the reader that the book is based upon research about the EMP threat, including reports of the United States EMP Commission.

The terrifying depiction of the aftermath of a nuclear EMP attack became a bestseller and was cited in the halls of Congress as recommended reading for all Americans. Yet perhaps most shocking of all is the fact that in the intervening years since the book was published in 2009, little to nothing has been accomplished by way of mitigating this mortal threat to the nation.

The United States government has in fact for decades been aware of the potentially cataclysmic threat to the nation's electrical power grid—yet despite reports and commissions galore, the nation's vital electrical grid remains vulnerable to a nuclear EMP attack.

There has been no shortage of legislation; however, bills to protect the nation's power grid that were passed unanimously by the House of Representatives—including the GRID Act, the Shield Act and the Critical Infrastructure Act—all died in the Senate.[6] Observers blame the electrical power industry for being unwilling to face up to the threat and expend the necessary resources to secure the nation's power grid.

Too Little Too Late?

In October 2015, after years of inaction and obfuscation in Washington, the White House released its long-awaited plan to prepare for a colossal EMP event. The *National Space Weather*

Action Plan was a complex strategy requiring cooperation among various government agencies. The six-step "Action Plan" requires the partnership of a bewildering "network of governments, agencies, emergency managers, academia, the media, the insurance industry, nonprofit organizations, and the private sector."[7] As one incredulous commentator put it: "In other words: We might be doomed."

The plan was arguably replete with bureaucratic verbiage and short on action. Most disappointing was the failure to compel the electrical energy industry to take concrete steps to protect the power grid. Instead, the plan spoke of *encouraging* "owners and operators of infrastructure and technology assets to coordinate development of realistic power-restoration priorities and expectations."[8]

Critics charge that this is akin to letting the foxes guard the henhouse. In a scathing indictment of the power industry, Woolsey points out the White House plan

> trusts NERC (North American Electric Reliability Corporation) and the electric utilities to set the standards. Nor has the White House or the U.S. FERC (Federal Energy Regulatory Commission) challenged NERC's assertion that it has no responsibility to protect the electric grid from nuclear EMP or Radio-Frequency Weapons. Nor has the White House or the U.S. FERC done anything to prevent NERC and the utilities from misinforming policymakers and the public about the EMP threat and their lack of preparedness to survive and recover from an EMP catastrophe.[9]

Iran Prepares for Cybergeddon?

Not surprisingly, foes of the United States have taken note of our lack of preparation against a nuclear EMP attack. An article in an Iranian political-military journal affirmed that such a weapon was the key to defeating the U.S. The article, entitled "Electronics to Determine Fate of Future Wars," predicted: "If the world's industrial countries fail to devise effective ways to defend themselves against dangerous electronic assaults, then they will disintegrate within a few years."[10]

The article was as much a threat as a warning, as intelligence experts report that both North Korea and Iran have practiced the iconic nuclear EMP attack against the United States using several different delivery systems—none of which is easy to counter.

The first is already flying overhead: North Korea's KSM-3 satellite orbits the U.S. on the optimum trajectory and altitude to evade our National Missile Defense (NMD). If fitted with a nuclear warhead, the KSM-3 would be positioned to create an EMP field over all 48 contiguous United States.[11] In November 2013 South Korea's intelligence service reported to the South Korea Parliament that North Korea had "purchased Russian electromagnetic pulse (EMP) weaponry to develop its own version" of a nuclear EMP device.[12]

As we noted above, Pyongyang reportedly also has the ability to fire nuclear-tipped weapons from mobile ICBM launchers that can reach the continental United States. Admiral Gortney conceded that it would be "very difficult" for the U.S. to counter the threat because it is unable to track the missiles and give an efficient warning before they are launched: "The KN-08 is a road-capable, highly mobile ICBM, which can be hidden anywhere throughout North Korea and could be fired on a short-countdown virtually undetectable by American intelligence."[13]

Both North Korea and Iran have also practiced yet another means of delivering a nuclear EMP using short-range missiles launched off cargo ships. This is no idle threat: In 2014 Iranian warships were detected patrolling in international waters off the U.S. Atlantic coast, an unprecedented maneuver that raised concerns that the Islamic state was making a dry run for an

EMP attack. Peter Vincent Pry, executive director of the EMP Task Force on National and Homeland Security, voiced the opinion that the presence of the Iranian ships was intended to lull the U.S. Navy into complacency.

According to Pry, any attack would likely be launched from a container freighter. Iran has acquired Russian Club-K missile launchers, which can be transported on cargo ships: "The Club-K is a complete missile launch system, disguised to look like a shipping container, that could convert any freighter into a missile launch platform," warns Pry. "The Club-K, if armed with a nuclear warhead, could be used to execute an EMP attack."[14]

This concern is heightened by reports that Iran has been practicing on the Caspian Sea, sending medium-range missiles two hundred miles above the surface of the earth—the optimum altitude for an EMP attack—using cargo container ships as a launching platform.

It is sobering to realize that—in contradistinction to the classic Cold War scenario of scores of nuclear missiles raining down upon U.S. cities—an EMP attack requires only a single nuclear weapon detonated in the skies above to immobilize the United States—or any nation. Woolsey warns that such a warhead detonated over the eastern U.S. would collapse the electrical grid:

> The Eastern Grid generates 75 percent of U.S. electricity and supports most of the national population. Such an attack could be made by a short-range Scud missile launched off a freighter, by a jet fighter or small private jet doing a zoom climb, or even by a meteorological balloon.[15]

Four Horsemen

Complicating matters is the fact that a nuclear EMP is only one possible threat to the United States. A Department of Energy

142

report examined four main risk scenarios that could threaten the nation's electrical grid:

1. A physical attack on electricity system equipment that disabled difficult-to-replace equipment in multiple generating stations or substations and caused a prolonged outage;

2. A coordinated cyberattack that impaired the integrity of multiple control systems;

3. A severe geomagnetic disturbance (GMD) that damaged difficult-to-replace generating station and substation equipment and caused a cascading effect on the system; and

4. A potential widespread pandemic influenza that resulted in the loss of critical personnel.[16]

The Department of Energy report touts the modest increase in U.S. production of LPTs, but fails to address the fact that, in the wake of an attack, domestic transformer production would be functionally nonexistent.

Enduring damage could be inflicted by the failure of a surprisingly few key grid components. The *Wall Street Journal* cites a study by the U.S. Federal Energy Regulatory Commission warning that a terrorist attack that destroys just nine key transformer substations could cause a nationwide blackout lasting eighteen months.[17]

Cyberattack

It is not necessary to launch a nuclear weapon in the sky overhead to send a nation into the Dark Ages: The same devastating results can be accomplished by cyberterrorists hunched over computer screens from virtually anywhere on the planet.

Cyberattack—a term unknown before 1988—has morphed into a scourge that is afflicting businesses and governments worldwide. A study by the consulting firm Pricewaterhouse-Coopers found that in 2014 the number of cyberattacks had skyrocketed to 42.8 million—or some 117,339 each day.[18]

Virtually every company surveyed reported being hit by cyberattack, causing hundreds of thousands and millions of dollars. The number of companies and organizations reporting a $20 million loss due to cyberattacks has nearly doubled since 2013. In one highly publicized example, as a result of a data breach during the 2013 holiday season, the retail giant Target Corporation was forced to shell out nearly $150 million to compensate customers for costs incurred.

As costly as cyberattacks are, they pale in comparison to their more nefarious cousin: cyberwarfare. While the damage caused by cyberattacks is generally limited to single companies, cyberwarfare is aimed at crippling an entire country. It can disrupt or shut down essential services such as the electrical network or the distribution of food and water. Cyberwarfare can bring down a nation's financial system and disable official communications.

In *Lights Out: A Cyberattack, A Nation Unprepared, Surviving the Aftermath*, journalist Ted Koppel argues that a terrorist assault on America's power grid would have devastating consequences—and shockingly that such an attack is not only possible but likely.[19] Not only major powers such as Russia and China but terrorism-linked nations such as North Korea and Iran are believed to be preparing cyberattacks.

As with an EMP attack, according to Koppel the United States has no strategy for responding to cyberwarfare: "There are plans for hurricanes, there are plans for snowstorms, there are plans for earthquakes. There is no plan for a cyberattack. . . ."[20] Even though numerous high-level officials have warned about a "cyber Pearl Harbor" affecting tens of millions, the response of the government has been a collective bureaucratic big yawn.

A Clear and Present Danger

Widespread blackouts are already happening. In April 2015 Washington, D.C., was hit by power outages that affected much of the city, including the White House, the Congress and the Metro public transport system, prompting media commentary about the vulnerability of the electric grid. The blackout reportedly was caused by a malfunction in a transformer substation.

The week prior to the Washington blackout, Turkey experienced a nationwide blackout by causes still unknown. Earlier in the year, 80 percent of Pakistan—a nuclear weapons nation—was blacked out by a terrorist attack. In June of 2014 the lights went out across the entire nation of Yemen after al Qaeda attacked the electric grid. Eighteen cities were blacked out, leaving 24 million people in the dark. Even criminal gangs have the ability to take down the electric grid: In 2013 the Knights Templar Cartel in Mexico cut the electrical supply to 420,000 people in order to carry out the execution of politicians opposed to the drug trade.

In recent years there has been a dramatic increase in attempts to damage the U.S. electric grid, as reported by *USA Today*: "Between 2011 and 2014, electric utilities reported 362 physical and cyberattacks that caused outages or other power disturbances to the U.S. Department of Energy. Of those, 14 were cyberattacks and the rest were physical in nature."[21]

Peter Pry summarizes how woefully unprepared the United States is despite years of warning:

The grid is utterly unprotected from an EMP attack. It's not adequately protected from cyber or physical sabotage. . . . It's why

North Korea and Iran want the bomb, have the bomb. North Korea has actually practiced this against the United States.[22]

X-Class Solar Storms

As incredible as it may seem, there exists an even greater threat than nuclear EMP or cyberwarfare attacks—one that could wipe out the technology and electric power grid not only of a single nation but of the entire planet. The term *solar storm* refers to planet Earth coming under attack from X rays, charged particles and magnetized plasma spewed from explosions on the surface of the sun. Solar flares occur frequently; most are too weak to cause damage.

It is the largest of these—monstrous X-class flares—that threaten our very existence. These mega-eruptions eject magnetized plasma into space with the force of a billion hydrogen bombs. Fortunately, CMEs shoot pretty much in a straight trajectory out from the sun, and given the vast reaches of space almost all miss the earth.

The first warning of one of these mega-eruptions will come from satellites operating a million miles away between the earth and the sun, operated jointly by NASA and the European Space Agency. These lonely sentinels are on the lookout for coronal mass ejections (CMEs) directed toward earth's orbit. From the moment the outpost satellites transmit the CME warning to NASA's Goddard Space Flight Center (GSFC) near Washington, D.C., the planet may have only hours before the cosmic tsunami hits.

What happens next is a series of unstoppable electrochemical reactions as the enormous cloud of plasma raining down from above generates huge electrical currents in the upper atmosphere that in turn trigger cataclysmic repercussions on the surface of the planet. As the geomagnetic solar storm hits the earth, the colossal surge of electricity will be absorbed by the electrical grid and power stations, melting the copper windings inside transformers.

It goes without saying that an X-class CME solar storm would bring our way of life to a grinding halt. The consequences for hundreds of millions of people suddenly going off the grid and competing for limited resources can scarcely be imagined.

There are historical examples of solar superstorms, such as the 1921 Railroad Storm, which occurred before America had a developed electric grid. Even so, over a period of two days the solar storm damaged or destroyed telephone, telegraph and cable equipment across the U.S. and much of Europe. Reports Woolsey: "The National Academy of Sciences estimates that if the Railroad Storm were to recur today, there would be a nationwide blackout with recovery requiring 4–10 years, if recovery is possible at all."[23]

The Carrington Event

We are now venturing to describe a global nightmare that defies comprehension. The most powerful space weather event on record occurred in 1859 when an extraordinarily powerful solar coronal mass ejection struck the earth's magnetosphere. The Carrington Event, named after the English astronomer who witnessed it, was estimated to be some ten times more powerful than the 1921 Railroad Storm and one hundred times more powerful than the 1989 Québec Blackout, a solar storm that caused the collapse of the province's electricity transmission system.

The effects of the 1859 Carrington Event were felt worldwide, producing several days of spectacular auroral displays. Telegraph stations burned, with wires exploding off their poles, causing forest fires. The newly laid intercontinental telegraph cable at the bottom of the Atlantic Ocean was rendered useless.

In short, the Carrington Event heavily damaged the primitive electric infrastructure that existed at the time.

What would be the effects of a present-day event of the same magnitude? Woolsey answers the question: "If a solar super-storm like the Carrington Event recurred today, it would collapse electric grids and life-sustaining critical infrastructures worldwide, putting at risk the lives of billions."[24]

The human and material costs of such an event are almost too fantastic to contemplate. Researchers from Lloyd's of London and Atmospheric and Environmental Research in the United States used data from the Carrington Event to estimate the current cost of a similar event to the U.S. alone at $0.6–2.6 trillion.[25] A study by the National Research Council of the National Academies came to a similar figure, with "an estimate of $1 trillion to $2 trillion during the first year alone . . . for the societal and economic costs of a 'severe geomagnetic storm scenario' with recovery times of 4 to 10 years."[26]

Up to ten years without electricity to provide us with food, water, transportation and a thousand other things essential to our lives? How many of us would be left?

A Near Miss

Well, at least we don't have to worry about solar flares—not in our lifetime, right? Wrong. According to physicist Pete Riley, senior scientist at Predictive Science in San Diego, California, there is an astounding 1 in 8 chance that the earth will be the target of an enormous mega flare from the sun *in the next decade*. This solar storm would rival the Carrington Event and could cause trillions of dollars in damage. The U.S. could take up to a decade to recover from such a catastrophe.[27]

Those who still imagine that such a scenario is the stuff of fantasy might be unnerved to learn that on July 23, 2012, a coronal mass ejection of exceptional strength on the scale of a Carrington Event tore through the earth's orbit. Fortunately, our planet was not there, having passed by with mere days to spare. A week earlier and the solar storm would have hit us full force.

A week earlier and exceedingly few of us would be left to read this page. The cost of the ensuing damage, once again, would have been in the trillions of dollars, with recovery taking many years. "If it had hit," says Daniel Baker, director of the Laboratory for Atmospheric and Space Physics of the University of Colorado, "we would still be picking up the pieces. How many other [storms] of this scale have just happened to miss Earth and our space detection systems? This is a pressing question that needs answers."[28]

The distressing truth is that in the years since 9/11, despite the dire warnings of experts and unsuccessful attempts at legislation, virtually nothing has been done to secure our vulnerable electrical grid, electronics, communications and distribution infrastructures. The United States—and perhaps the world—is plowing headlong toward utter catastrophe.

The terrifying destruction in Revelation said to take place "in an hour" is no longer a perplexing reference glossed over by commentators, but a very real possibility that grows more likely with each passing day. Woolsey minces no words:

> EMP is a clear and present danger, and . . . something must be done to protect the electric grid and other life sustaining critical infrastructures—immediately. . . . Continued inaction by Washington will make inevitable a natural or manmade EMP catastrophe.[29]

As to exactly how a massive EMP event—natural or manmade—could play a role in biblical prophecy, there are a number of admittedly speculative and unthinkable possibilities. One scenario envisions the entire planet being crippled by a CME solar storm that causes social and political chaos, preparing the way for a charismatic leader who promises to restore order and peace to a shattered world. This scenario could explain how nations seemingly offer so little resistance to the nefarious program of the Beast of Revelation, also known as the Antichrist.

Another possibility is that an EMP attack specifically against the United States renders this nation incapable of involvement in the end time events. Such a scenario would comport with the identification of Mystery Babylon as America, which experiences sudden destruction.

A License to Oppress

In the Olivet Discourse, Jesus speaks to His disciples about calamitous events that will occur at the end of time: "There will be great earthquakes, famines and pestilences in various places, and fearful events and great signs from heaven" (Luke 21:11). It is easy to imagine an EMP attack or a solar superstorm such as we have described being among the "fearful events" that result in "famines and pestilences."

Jesus then stipulates, however, that prior to the onset of these earth-shaking events something will occur that triggers the final countdown: "But before all this, they will seize you and persecute you." Jesus' disciples will be "brought before kings and governors" and put in prison "all on account of my name" (verse 12). The mention of being "brought before" the authorities and "put in prison" indicates that one day Jesus' disciples will be arrested, charged with breaking the law, duly convicted and incarcerated for their "crimes."

In the first centuries after Christ, the followers of Jesus were arrested, imprisoned and on many occasions martyred for various "crimes," notably that of "impiety" or atheism— the refusal to pay homage to the Roman pantheon of gods.

But Western societies are not polytheistic and do not demand that their citizens bow before idols. This leads to the question, How could such an appalling state of affairs ever come about—especially in Western Christendom with its tradition of freedom of worship and belief in the rule of law based upon Scriptural principles?

Such a sea change of sentiment toward Christians foretold by Jesus could come about through a fundamental transformation of society leading to the institution of laws that brand people of faith as "lawbreakers" subject to punishment. Such a scenario, once unimaginable in Western Christendom, is fast becoming an Orwellian reality in a growing number of countries.

The fulcrum that threatens to bring wholesale legal persecution upon Christians is this: the charge that those who hold to the biblical view of marriage and sexuality are "intolerant" and guilty of "hate crimes." The prophet Isaiah issues a sharp rebuke to those who overturn the divinely ordained moral order: "Woe to those who call evil good and good evil, who put darkness for light and light for darkness" (Isaiah 5:20).

The resulting moral confusion and disintegration brings weakness to a nation, as recognized by former-President Ronald Reagan, who, quoting Dwight Eisenhower and others, stated that "America is great because America is good. And if America ever stops being good, America will stop being great." In such a state of rebellion the United States could no longer hope for God's blessing and would be reduced to an impotent nation both unable and unwilling to stand with Israel against her foes.

Later in the same chapter Isaiah goes on to forecast a sudden destruction of those who "call evil good and good evil" that resembles the fate of Mystery Babylon:

> Therefore the LORD's anger burns against his people; his hand
> is raised and he strikes them down. The mountains shake, and
> the dead bodies are like refuse in the streets. . . . In that day they

will roar over it like the roaring of the sea. And if one looks at the land, there is only darkness and distress; even the sun will be darkened by clouds.

Isaiah 5:25, 30

The one great characteristic of Mystery Babylon that the United States does not yet exhibit is the wholesale persecution of believers: "In her was found the blood of prophets and of God's holy people" (Revelation 18:24). But that could all change—and sooner than we realize.

We will now explore how the rejection of biblical teaching on human sexuality could be the one enormous weapon of evil that knocks America from her godly foundations—and which could seal her identification as the Mystery Babylon of Revelation.

11

The Criminalization
of Christianity

In 1796, as he prepared to leave the president's office and return to Mount Vernon to spend his remaining years with his beloved wife, Martha, George Washington composed his farewell address to the nation that he had served faithfully for more than four decades.

In his address Washington called for the continued centrality of religion and morality in the life of the nation. He rejected the notion that morality can be maintained without religion—and in Washington's time "religion" could scarcely refer to anything other than America's Judeo-Christian heritage. In what many have taken as a prescient look into the future, Washington expressed doubt that any "sincere friend" of the country could "look with indifference upon attempts to shake the foundation of the [moral] fabric" of the nation:

Of all the dispositions and habits which lead to political prosperity, religion and morality are indispensable supports. In vain would that man claim the tribute of patriotism, who should labor to subvert these great pillars of human happiness, these firmest props of the duties of men and citizens. The mere politician, equally with the pious man, ought to respect and to cherish them. A volume could not trace all their connections with private and public felicity. Let it simply be asked: Where is the security for property, for reputation, for life, if the sense of religious obligation desert the oaths which are the instruments of investigation in courts of justice? And let us with caution indulge the supposition that morality can be maintained without religion. Whatever may be conceded to the influence of refined education on minds of peculiar structure, reason and experience both forbid us to expect that national morality can prevail in exclusion of religious principle.

It is substantially true that virtue or morality is a necessary spring of popular government. The rule, indeed, extends with more or less force to every species of free government. Who that is a sincere friend to it can look with indifference upon attempts to shake the foundation of the fabric?[1]

George Washington would be aghast to witness the cultural and moral transformation—the very "shaking of the foundation" as it were—that America is undergoing today. The race to ostracize and eventually criminalize certain beliefs that have constituted the nation's moral order since the time of our Founding Fathers—as well as all of Christendom before them—is quickening at an alarming pace. As we shall see, people of faith are already being threatened with jail time and draconian fines for holding to their beliefs. Should our nation continue along this dangerous path, we could find ourselves fulfilling the prophecy about Mystery Babylon, which "was drunk with the blood of God's holy people, the blood of those who bore testimony to Jesus" (Revelation 17:6).

154

Jail Time for Believers

In September 2015 viewers of televised news broadcasts watched a recorded spectacle that even a few months earlier would have been inconceivable: A duly elected county clerk in Kentucky was arrested by U.S. Marshals and escorted handcuffed to a detention facility for the "crime" of refusing—in accordance with state law—to issue marriage certificates to homosexual couples.

The last thing Rowan County Clerk Kim Davis says she wanted was to be thrust into the national spotlight. As a dedicated Christian, she had come to faith later in life after going through many troubles, including failed marriages. She felt constrained to take a stand rather than allow her name to be affixed to certificates of marriage for homosexual couples. Davis based her decision on what she believed was her First Amendment freedom of religion.

Davis would be portrayed by many in the media as an obstinate Bible-thumping right-wing fanatic who hated gays and lesbians and was intent upon denying them their constitutional rights, a charge she strongly denied: "I have no animosity toward anyone and harbor no ill will. To me this has never been a gay or lesbian issue. It is about marriage and God's Word. It is a matter of religious liberty. . . ."[2]

A federal judge ordered Davis jailed for contempt of court for refusing to comply with his order to issue the licenses. The judge dismissed the clerk's appeal to her First Amendment rights, including freedom of religion and the free exercise of religion. Televised news broadcasts showed her being taken handcuffed into custody by U.S. Marshals because of her refusal to sanction what she considered to be a morally objectionable lifestyle.

Many of the media reports failed to mention key facts in the case. Davis was acting in accordance with the laws of Kentucky, which she had sworn to uphold. According to the State of Kentucky Revised Statutes (chapter 402.005) marriage is defined as between "one (1) man and one (1) woman united in law for life." The same section specifically prohibits marriage between members of the same sex. In a statewide referendum in 2004, the electorate in Kentucky affirmed the definition of marriage as between a man and a woman, passing a constitutional amendment by an overwhelming three-to-one margin.

Also generally unreported was Davis' request that the Kentucky marriage license forms be revised so that her name would not appear on them. She stated that she would duly record any license so long as it did not have her name affixed, as she did not wish to be seen as approving of homosexual marriage.

This compromise failed to sway the judge, who then decreed that licenses issued by Davis' deputy clerks would be valid even without her signature. Critics professed amazement at the judge's action, pointing out that he could just as easily have granted Davis' request to change the forms not to include her name.

"Freedom" of Religion?

This is not an isolated case. People of biblical faith who do not want to service homosexual marriages are being brought more and more frequently before extrajudicial "hate crimes" tribunals and fined. The dam has broken and the attack is on full bore. For the dark forces that have been biding their time, their opportunity has come. The dogs of war have been unleashed.

America is being recast primarily through the systematic undermining of its historic understanding regarding marriage and the family. The advancement of homosexuality and what has come to be known as the "gay agenda" have been the tip of the spear in this fight against traditional values. Federal policies have been overhauled to provide benefits to same-sex partners and make high-profile appointments of gays and lesbians to the judiciary and the executive branches. The "Don't Ask, Don't Tell" fiat was nullified, thus ending the ban on gays serving in the military.

In the summer of 2015 the Pentagon announced that transgender Americans would also be allowed to serve in the armed forces. The pace was accelerating: Also in 2015, in what was heralded as "a historic first," the first openly gay Secretary of the Army was nominated. Washington also took steps to promote its *cause célèbre* on the international scene with the appointment of the first-ever Special Envoy for Human Rights for LGBT (lesbian, gay, bisexual and transgender) persons.

The gay agenda received a tremendous boost in the wake of the U.S. Supreme Court *Obergefell v. Hodges* decision in June 2015 legalizing homosexual marriage. Seemingly deaf to the concerns of millions of Americans who strongly disagreed with the controversial decision, the White House had filed a brief with the Supreme Court in support of the petitioning homosexuals and was lighted up in rainbow colors in celebration of the decision.

The Supreme Court's redefinition of marriage served to accelerate the attacks upon those who attempted to make a stand for traditional marriage. In a landmark case a Colorado appellate court ruled that an evangelical Christian owner of a cake shop in Denver was guilty of violating the rights of a gay couple when he declined on religious grounds to bake a custom wedding cake for them.

And the rights of the cake shop owner? The court rejected the defendant's claim that being forced to service a homosexual wedding "violates their constitutional rights to freedom of speech and the free exercise of religion."[3] The bakery owner was ordered to take "remedial measures" including "comprehensive staff training" explaining how the First Amendment did not apply to their religious beliefs. In a final jackbooted insult, the court required the hapless owner to file "quarterly compliance reports" to ensure that there would be no reversion to the former discriminatory ways.

In another controversial decision, the commissioner of the Oregon Bureau of Labor and Industries upheld a $135,000 fine against the Christian owners of another small bakery for the offense of declining to provide a wedding cake for a lesbian commitment ceremony. The lesbian couple was awarded the damages "for emotional and mental suffering resulting from the denial of service." In the 122-page decision, the commissioner rejected the First Amendment freedom of religion defense of the bakery owners as "entirely lacking in merit."[4]

In a shocking breach of judicial etiquette, it was revealed that the commissioner had regular meetings with a gay rights advocacy group while publicly supporting the lesbians' case. The defense attorney accused the commissioner of being

> outspoken throughout this case about his intent to "rehabilitate" those whose beliefs do not conform to the state's ideas. The judge, jury and executioner are all in one place. He is intent on using his office to root out thought and speech with which he personally disagrees.[5]

In addition to the ruinous financial penalties, the commissioner imposed a gag order demanding that the husband and wife owners cease and desist from making public statements regarding their opposition to the decision. Gay rights groups launched protests and picketed the bakery. After the children of the owners reportedly received death threats, the bakery closed, and the father was forced to take a job as a trash collector to support his family of five.

The *New York Times* has cited numerous cases of people coming under fire because of their religious convictions, including a Christian couple in New York who were fined $13,000 for declining to rent out their farmhouse for a lesbian wedding. The *Times* cites other examples of those charged with violating "antidiscrimination" laws for refusing to provide wedding services to homosexuals, including

> a photographer in New Mexico, a florist in Washington State, a bakery in Oregon, an inn in Vermont and wedding chapels in Idaho and in Nevada. And new cases continue to arise—over the last few weeks, a wedding planner in Arizona declined to work with a lesbian couple, and a business in California refused to photograph the wedding of a gay male couple (and then closed its doors after an outcry).[6]

The Fired Fire Chief

The repercussions for Christians who speak against the gay agenda—even in their private lives—are becoming more extensive. Atlanta's highly decorated Fire Chief Kelvin Cochran discovered the hard way that tolerance is not always granted to people of faith. After he was awarded Fire Chief of the Year in 2012, Mayor Kasim Reed praised him: "Chief Cochran's pioneering efforts to improve performance and service within the Atlanta Fire Rescue Department have won him much-deserved national recognition."

That was before Chief Cochran wrote and self-published a book on his own time to encourage the young men he ministered to at Atlanta's Elizabeth Baptist Church, where he serves as a deacon and leads a men's Bible study. The book explains how the teachings of Christ can empower men to be responsible husbands and fathers. Mr. Cochran's offense was a few passages stating that homosexuality is contrary to the Bible and a perversion of the natural order.

Mayor Reed summarily suspended his chief without pay for thirty days before firing him, claiming that

Chief Cochran's book is not representative of my personal beliefs, and is inconsistent with the administration's work to make
Atlanta a more welcoming city for all of her citizens—regardless
of their sexual orientation, gender, race and religious beliefs.[7]

Alex Wan, an openly gay member of the city council, implied
that freedom of religion did not extend to public employees:
"I respect each individual's right to have their own thoughts,
beliefs and opinions, but when you're a city employee, and those
thoughts, beliefs and opinions are different from the city's, you
have to check them at the door."[8]

Before publishing the book, Chief Cochran had contacted the
city's ethics department and received permission to pursue the
project despite the fact that there is no official requirement to
obtain authorization to write a book on one's own time. David
Cortman of Alliance Defending Freedom, who is defending Mr.
Cochran, says the city is "using protocol arguments to cover
its tracks after wrongly terminating someone for holding and
expressing religious views that city officials didn't like."[9]

Following a court hearing, Chief Cochran issued a statement
that gave voice to increasing numbers of people who fear the
growing criminalization of Christianity:

> Our nation was founded on the principle that everyone should
> be free to not just believe what they want, but to live their lives
> according to those beliefs. I'm here today not just for myself,
> but for every religious person in America who does not want
> to live in fear of facing termination for expressing their faith.[10]

These shocking examples of the overreach of judicial power
remind us once again of Jesus' forewarning that before the com-
mencement of the end time calamities His disciples would be
brought before the authorities of the state and suffer persecution. If the United States persists down the path of trampling
underfoot its Christian heritage, our great nation will disqualify

itself from the honor of standing with Israel against the assault of Gog and Magog.

The Eradication of Male and Female

The next logical milestone of the sexual revolution—after establishing that the sex of one's marital spouse is interchangeable—appears to be the denial of any essential differences between male and female. This is evident in the redefinition of a key term: *gender*. Older dictionaries such as *Webster's Ninth New Collegiate Dictionary* give as the primary definition simply "(biological) sex." The online *Webster's Dictionary* defines *gender* unambiguously as "the state of being male or female."

In the 1950s sexologist Dr. John Money was instrumental in redefining the word *gender* from meaning one's biological sex to meaning one's subjective identification. Money had an ulterior motive: For many years he performed controversial sex-change operations at Johns Hopkins University until the practice was stopped because of concerns about negative outcomes in the patients. The new definition was picked up by feminist theorists in the 1970s and later was used by gay activists intent on reshaping societal views toward the acceptance of homosexuality.

In recognition of the movement to redefine the term, OxfordDictionaries.com—created by the publishers of *The Oxford English Dictionary*—added the ambiguous prefix "Mx." (pronounced *mix*) as an option to "Mr.," "Mrs." and "Ms." in the dictionary. One admittedly sexually ambiguous individual who welcomed the new designation stated:

> The addition of Mx to the dictionary represents the beginning of an unprecedented shift in how Western language, thought and culture understands gender. By adding Mx, the editors embraced a future in which gender does not have to be limited to

two options: a world where people can determine their gender on their own terms.[11]

This new understanding of the word *gender* is reflected in the latest *Oxford Dictionary,* which states that the term is "typically used with reference to social and cultural differences rather than biological ones."

The transgender movement is based upon this radical new definition of *gender* as one's personal identification as male or female irrespective of biological sex. The *Obergefell v. Hodges* decision provided impetus for this new understanding, allowing states and municipalities to implement antidiscrimination laws and policies targeting those who opposed homosexuality and transgenderism.

This constitutes rebellion against the very order of creation set forth in Genesis: "So God created mankind in his own image, in the image of God he created them; male and female he created them" (Genesis 1:27).

Here we see the sinister hand of the evil one—the hater of all that is good—who tempted Adam and Eve in the Garden with the lie: "You will be like God, knowing good and evil" (Genesis 3:5). Instead of submitting to the divine authority, those who persist in rebellion become "a law unto themselves" (Romans 2:14 KJV), pretending to be capable of deciding for themselves even that most fundamental of human characteristics: male and female.

As a nation we are edging toward the fate of Mystery Babylon, who was consumed with "abominations and filthiness" (Revelation 17:4 KJV). How long can it be before we plunge into the abyss?

The Unmelting Pot

In what appears to be blatant partiality, the U.S. government is vigorously engaged in protecting the rights of religious peoples—except for Christians, it seems. At the same time County Clerk Kim Davis was being jailed for refusing to perform actions in contradiction to her religious beliefs, the U.S. Equal Employment Opportunity Commission (EEOC) was considering the complaint of a Muslim flight attendant who was suspended from her job for refusing to serve alcohol to her flight passengers. Given its recent decisions, it is likely that the EEOC will rule in her favor.

In 2013 the EEOC sued a trucking company, Star Transport, for terminating two Muslims who refused to deliver alcohol even though the beverages were in sealed containers and the drivers had no direct contact with it. In its court filings, the EEOC cited the requirement of employers to provide "reasonable accommodation": "Failure to accommodate the religious beliefs of employees, when this can be done without undue hardship, violates Title VII of the Civil Rights Act of 1964 which prohibits discrimination on the basis of religion."[12] The EEOC won $240,000 in damages for the drivers.

In other cases, the EEOC sued Alamo Rent A Car after the company fired a Muslim employee for wearing a headscarf. The woman was awarded $250,000 in punitive damages. The Muslim workers of a subsidiary of Heinz Foods filed a complaint with the EEOC alleging that the company was discriminating against them. The company had, in fact, provided two prayer rooms, but balked when the Muslim employees insisted upon leaving the production line to pray outside of designated break times.

Muslim taxi drivers at the Minneapolis International Airport have appealed to the EEOC after being terminated for refusing to transport passengers carrying alcohol in their luggage. Muslim employees of Hertz, Walmart, Target, Disney and a host of other American businesses have successfully sued for special accommodation. The notion of moving beyond reasonable accommodation and creating special rights for a special class of people is in accordance with the Islamic belief that Muslims are superior to the *kuffar* or unbeliever.

Freedom of religion in the workplace has been an inviolable tenet of American jurisprudence. According to John Hendrickson, the EEOC regional attorney for the Chicago District Office:

> Everyone has a right to observe his or her religious beliefs, and employers don't get to pick and choose which religions and which religious practices they will accommodate. If an employer can reasonably accommodate an employee's religious practice without an undue hardship, then it must do so. That is a principle which has been memorialized in federal employment law for almost 50 years.[13]

Alarmingly, however, in the growing numbers of cases of Christians being subjected to lawsuits—and now jail time—the principle of reasonable accommodation, such as Clerk Davis and many others have requested, and which is supposedly "memorialized in federal employment law," is ignored.

It is not unreasonable to fear that the juggernaut to marginalize Christians could soon lead to open persecution. A tenuous and hotly debated "religious exemption" clause was all that kept churches and religious organizations from being found in violation of antidiscrimination and hate crime laws. Many Christians feared that they were one court decision away from fines against religious institutions that refuse to marry same-sex couples or refuse to hire open homosexuals, followed by the padlocking of offending churches and the jailing of pastors. The warning of Jesus regarding the persecution of believers before the end of time may find its fulfillment in our time.

And where does the quest for inclusivity end? Is it really inconceivable that companies in the future might be required to administer tests to prospective employees in order to ensure that they do not hold dangerous "reactionary attitudes"? Will

Christians who resist the encroachment of nontraditional values be branded more and more as hatemongers? Will re-education camps for offenders become a reality?

But as the night is darkest just before the first rays of dawn, indications have begun to appear that perhaps all is not lost. Just perhaps the true haters—those who despise God's truth—will overplay their hand as they have so often in times past. There is hope that our great land will yet pull back from the brink and will escape the fate of Mystery Babylon.

Theologians have for millennia debated the relationship between God's sovereignty and human freedom, with differing schools of thought emphasizing either divine sovereignty or free will. Here is a great mystery, for while God's all-surpassing power and control over events is undeniable, at the same time throughout the Scriptures humans are admonished to exercise their will:

> "Choose for yourselves this day whom you will serve, whether the gods your ancestors served beyond the Euphrates, or the gods of the Amorites, in whose land you are living. But as for me and my household, we will serve the LORD."
>
> Joshua 24:15

The United States and its citizens are approaching the point of decision. Yes, God has a plan, but we are commanded to choose to obey Him—and those decisions, individually and collectively, will reveal what role the United States will play in the unfolding end time events.

There are indeed rays of hope breaking across the increasingly bleak landscape—signs that growing numbers of Americans are awakening from their slumber and standing up against the great rebellion that rejects God-created male and female distinctions.

12

Darkest Before the Dawn

After the landmark Supreme Court decision mandating the acceptance of homosexual marriage in America, it appeared that the movement to overturn traditional views about sexuality had triumphed. Polls indicating greater acceptance of homosexuality, especially with the younger generation, were trumpeted as proof that the old, repressive morality would eventually die out.

That is why the unexpected protests against the demands of transsexuals at a Missouri high school—led by teenagers no less—constituted a shot across the bow to the proponents of the new pansexuality. Many of the students at Hillsboro High School took a "live and let live" attitude toward gays and transsexuals—that is, until they began to experience the ramifications of the movement to grant special rights and privileges to those lifestyles.

"Lila" Perry was a young homosexual male who had come out as transgender during his junior year and began dressing as a female. When school administrators were made aware of Lila's new sexual identity and intention to use the female bathrooms and locker room, they offered him the use of a unisex faculty bathroom in an attempt to defuse the situation. Lila felt that being confined to the unisex bathroom was unacceptable and demanded full access to the women's bathrooms and locker and shower rooms.

The high school administration felt forced to acquiesce in the face of the support for transgender rights that comes from the highest reaches of the United States government. The U.S. Department of Education's Office for Civil Rights (OCR), for instance, has issued guidelines regarding "harassment and discriminatory treatment of a transgender student."[1] The OCR has made evident that school districts must comply with the "vigorous enforcement" of the new policy protecting transgender students.

As part of its agreement to settle the Missouri case, the OCR required the school district to treat the male transgender "the same as other female students in all respects in the education programs and activities offered by the District, including access to sex-designated facilities for female students."[2]

When Lila began showing up in the women's facilities, however, much of the carefully nurtured political correctness to accept transgenderism as "just another lifestyle choice" collided with the brick wall of reality. In other circumstances the appearance of a male student in the women's bathroom or locker room would be cause for expulsion. Now a biologically male student dressed in women's clothing and wearing a wig—who had not undergone gender reassignment surgery—was permitted to undress, use toilet facilities and shower alongside female students.

The controversy soon had the community up in arms: During a packed school board meeting concerns were voiced that "the transgender student was getting 'special rights' at the expense of the other teens at the school. Parents were upset that the privacy rights of their daughters would be violated if forced to share a bathroom or locker room with a genetic male."[3] The *St. Louis Post Dispatch* reported a poll showing that students and parents were "overwhelmingly in support of keeping Lila . . . out of the school facilities for girls."[4]

The madness of the school's policy was a stunning wakeup call for many students who until that moment had taken pride in their "progressive" stance toward transgenders and other "sexual minorities." Now, suddenly, they were brought face-to-face with the stark reality of life in the Brave New World. Many female students, already self-conscious about undressing in front of other girls, were mortified at the thought of having to disrobe alongside a biological male.

Lila's determination to use the women's facilities sparked a mass walkout, with some two hundred students taking the unprecedented action of leaving their classrooms and protesting for two hours outside the school. Few parents in the rural community of Hillsdale were prepared to force their children to undress and use bathroom facilities in the presence of the opposite sex.

One parent of two daughters submitted a proposal to the board that students use the bathroom based on their anatomical sex or else use a "gender-neutral facility." CNN remarked that the proposal resonated with those present: "He's clearly not alone. His remarks at the school board meeting were greeted with thunderous applause and cheers."[5]

In another day the father's sensible idea would have passed without a second thought. But with the power and authority of the federal government committed to a societal transformation in lockstep with LGBT activists, school boards hesitate to implement commonsense privacy protections for their students for fear of losing federal funding—not to mention facing lawsuits.

The "experts" assure the public that expressing a transgender identity is a "healthy, appropriate and typical aspect of human development," and warn that forcing transgender students to use facilities consistent with their biological sex is "unethical" and likely to cause "significant emotional harm."[6] The unspoken threat is that failure to comply will likely result in expensive litigation.

The juggernaut to enforce the rights of transgenders to use bathroom and shower facilities of the opposite sex continues. Soon after the Missouri case, the DOE Office of Civil Rights threatened to pull federal funding from a school district in Illinois and backed a transgender girl's demand to use facilities for male students in Virginia.

The Illinois school district had attempted to compromise with a teenage boy who is biologically male but who identifies himself as female by providing him with a privacy curtain in the girl's locker room. The boy and his lawyers rejected the compromise, demanding unfettered access to the girls' locker room despite privacy and modesty concerns raised by parents of the girls.

District 211 Superintendent Daniel Cates voiced the objections of many: "At some point, we have to balance the privacy rights of 12,000 students" with the wishes of transsexuals. "We believe this infringes on the privacy of all the students that we serve." Cates called the decision of the federal government to force the school district to comply "a serious overreach with precedent-setting implications."[7]

The Sleeping Giant

In the wake of successes of the LGBT agenda, some in the Christian community counseled that "we need to move on—this issue is lost."

On the other hand, many Protestants and Catholics have shown themselves confident to speak out against the gay agenda. On the eve of the Supreme Court decision legalizing homosexual marriage, the Southern Baptist Convention, the largest Protestant denomination in the U.S., passed a resolution that spoke of the need to "extend respect in Christ's name to all people, including those who may disagree with us about the definition of marriage and the public good." The resolution went on to state: "No matter how the Supreme Court rules, the Southern Baptist Convention reaffirms its unwavering commitment to its doctrinal and public beliefs concerning marriage."[8]

SBC President Ronnie Floyd reminded members of the sixteen-million-member denomination of the words of Lutheran pastor and anti-Nazi dissident Dietrich Bonhoeffer, who warned: "Silence in the face of evil is itself evil. God will not hold us guiltless. Not to speak is to speak, and not to act is to act."[9] The church in the U.S. is facing a "Bonhoeffer Moment," said Floyd: "While some evangelicals . . . may be bowing down to the deception of the inclusiveness of same-sex marriage in their churches, we will not bow down, nor will we be silent."[10]

In the aftermath of the Supreme Court decision to legalize same-sex unions, a steady drumbeat of media reports observed that opposition to LGBT causes was steadily decreasing. It is only a matter of time, they claimed, before opposition to homosexual marriage would be viewed the same as the earlier resistance to interracial marriage, or giving women the right to vote.

As if on cue, a Pew Research Center study revealed that a "growing number" of religious bodies have chosen to accept same-sex unions, most notably the Episcopal Church, the Evangelical Lutheran Church in America, the Presbyterian Church (USA) and the United Church of Christ.[11]

A closer look, however, reveals surprising strength in the churches that still stand for traditional moral values. The study also acknowledged that "many of the largest U.S. religious institutions have remained firmly against allowing same-sex marriage."[12] These include the Roman Catholic Church, the Southern Baptist Convention and the Lutheran Church—Missouri Synod.

It is often implied that the two sides (those for and those against same-sex marriage), are roughly equal in size. Nothing could be further from the truth. When the actual membership of the various religious institutions, Christian and non-Christian, is compared, a different picture altogether emerges.

The Pew Research Center report listed seven church denominations and one Jewish group that accepted homosexual marriage, with a combined membership of some 11.5 million congregants. By comparison, the report listed six church denominations plus one Jewish group, Islamists and Mormons as opposing gay unions. The total membership of these religious organizations was nearly 105 million adherents—or nine times the membership of pro-gay-marriage religious groups.

There is more: A report by the Hartford Institute for Religion Research entitled "Fast Facts about American Religion" listed the top 25 church groups in the U.S.[13] Only four of those groups are listed by the Pew Research Center as accepting homosexual marriage.

But even that is not the whole story. The Hartford Institute reported that "total church membership reported in the 2012 Yearbook is 145,691,446 members."[14] Since few if any other denominations have come out in favor of same-sex unions, this indicates that denominations representing fewer than 12 million out of more than 145 million congregants in the U.S have embraced the Supreme Court decision. The true number is far less, as the newly "gay friendly" churches contain significant numbers of parishioners who oppose the LGBT agenda but choose to maintain a silent witness in hopes that their churches will one day return to traditional biblical values.

The proponents of homosexual marriage often claim that history is on their side—"it's only a matter of time before homophobia is a relic of the past. . . ." We shall show how this assertion does not accord with the historical data. But first, by way of definition, denominations that have accepted same-sex unions are known as "liberal" or "progressive" churches in the sense that over time they question or turn from traditional Christian beliefs and morals. Their acceptance of homosexual marriage is often the culmination of a long history of embracing unorthodox positions.

On the other side of the theological spectrum are "conservative" denominations, which hold to historic Christian teaching as expressed in the ancient creeds as well as to traditional moral beliefs. These churches reject the call to change with the times, but rather seek to "contend for the faith that was once for all entrusted to God's holy people" (Jude 1:3). In recent times the two most contentious ethical issues that have sharply divided liberal and conservative denominations are abortion and homosexuality.

In matters of religion people vote with their feet. Changes in the membership rolls of a church are typically indicative of either approval or disapproval on the part of congregants. The Hartford Institute data is revealing in that it shows that liberal denominations historically have lost members while conservative churches are growing.

In many cases the dichotomy is dramatic, with once-vibrant liberal churches losing members by the busloads. Since 1967 the Presbyterian Church USA has shrunk by 47 percent, the Episcopal Church has lost 49 percent of its congregants and the United Church of Christ has lost 52 percent of its congregants.[15]

The acceptance of same-sex unions has clearly been a significant factor in the hemorrhaging of members in liberal churches. In the two years after the Evangelical Lutheran Church of America (ELCA) voted by a narrow margin in 2009 to permit the ordination of noncelibate homosexuals and lesbians, the denomination lost fully 10 percent of its membership.[16] By contrast, the ELCA's sister denomination, the conservative Lutheran Congregations in Mission for Christ, has tripled the number of congregations on its roster—from 217 to 716—since the ELCA voted to ordain homosexuals and lesbians.

Many other conservative churches have also prospered. Since the mid-1960s the two largest Christian churches in the U.S. have experienced impressive growth: Membership in the Roman Catholic Church is up 49 percent and membership in the Southern Baptist Convention is up 46 percent. The group of major denominations listed as "Conservative Protestant" by the Hartford Institute report have grown by an average of 43 percent since the mid-'60s.

Another powerhouse group of denominations, the "Pentecostal and Holiness Protestant" churches, has on average experienced a remarkable 148 percent growth, led by the Church of God–Cleveland (+393%) and the world's largest Pentecostal church, the Assemblies of God (+430%).[17]

The "facts on the ground" belie the oft-repeated claim that homosexual marriage is gaining acceptance in the Christian community—which comprises the vast majority of the voting public. Yet there remain powerful forces determined to implement the radical LGBT agenda that threaten to compel people of faith to acquiesce or face harsh sanctions. Should they succeed, they may well prove correct those who argue that the United States meets the description of Mystery Babylon, a worldwide economic power that nonetheless revels in "abominations and filthiness" and ruthlessly persecutes believers who wish to remain faithful to God's Word.

But there is still hope. Let us examine an example of the silent majority standing up against unelected bureaucrats who attempted to force schools and businesses to allow transgendered people to undress, shower and share bathrooms with those of the opposite sex.

Showdown in Houston

In November 2015 attention was focused on the nation's fourth largest metropolitan area as a controversial homosexual rights ordinance with national implications was put to the vote. At root was the attempt by LGBT advocates to codify the elimination of intrinsic differences between male and female, replaced by a redefinition of "gender" to mean a person's subjective choice about whether that individual wishes to identify as male or female—or both.

Emboldened by various successes of the gay agenda, Annise Parker, the openly lesbian mayor of Houston, attempted to push through a radical nondiscrimination ordinance called the Houston Equal Rights Ordinance (HERO) despite legal objections.

The mayor said the ordinance was a personal battle about "my rights." She refused to submit the ordinance to a vote, asserting: "No one's rights should be subject to a popular vote."[18]

After the city council passed HERO, in an unprecedented and highly controversial move, Mayor Parker sought to silence prominent Houston pastors who opposed the ordinance by ordering city attorneys to subpoena their "sermons," "speeches" and other "communications" regarding "homosexuality, or gender identity."[19] After a public outcry that received national attention she was forced to back down. The Texas Supreme Court stepped in and ordered the city council either to repeal HERO or submit it to the voters for approval.

HERO was arguably one of the most extensive homosexual rights ordinances to be presented by a municipality in the U.S., making it illegal to discriminate based on fifteen different "projected characteristics." Dubbed the "Bathroom Bill" by opponents, the ordinance gave men and women who self-identify as transgendered access to any "place of public accommodation," including the bathrooms, shower rooms and locker rooms of the opposite sex. All Houston businesses would be required, for example, to make all women's facilities available to those who are dressed in female attire, without regard to biological sex.

Opponents of the bill argued that men dressed in feminine attire should not be granted access to women's facilities. Jared Woodfill, co-chair of the Campaign for Houston, which opposed the measure, laid out the stakes: "This [resolution] allows biological males, including registered sex offenders, to go into female restrooms, locker rooms and shower rooms all under the protection of law," he said. "We think that's dangerous public policy, and our position from day one has been we're not willing to sacrifice the safety of our wives, our daughters and our mothers at the altar of political correctness."[20]

HERO also refused private business owners the option of whether or not to participate in same-sex weddings, similar to the ordinances in other states that force bakers, florists, photographers, musicians and others to service homosexual marriages against their religious convictions.

The ordinance pushed the envelope even further, requiring Houston businesses to submit to the judgment of City Hall as to what qualities or characteristics are most relevant to a particular job. Critics feared that businesses would be forced to hire those who openly promote LGBT behavior that might be contrary to the owner's personal beliefs.

HERO was viewed as a test case for the next level of radical homosexual rights regulations and received high-profile endorsements from Hollywood celebrities and Fortune 500 companies including Apple, General Electric, Hewlett-Packard and Dow Chemical. The ordinance also received the backing of prominent politicians, including a statement of support from the White House.[21]

Major media outlets weighed in on the side of HERO, with the *New York Times* editorial board imploring the citizens of Houston not to "succumb to ugly fearmongering," stating that allowing transgender people to use bathrooms of the opposite biological sex "is a fundamental right that does nothing to endanger others."[22]

Well-heeled homosexual rights groups, such as the Human Rights Campaign, poured millions of dollars into the eighteen-month campaign, outspending groups opposed to the ordinance by three to one.

The LGBT tsunami appeared unstoppable. Polls taken before the vote predicted confidently that HERO would pass, and thus supporters were all the more flummoxed when the ordinance failed spectacularly by a margin of 62 to 38 percent.

Mayor Parker wasted no time in lashing out at opponents of the measure: "This was a campaign of fear-mongering and deliberate lies. . . . This is about a small group of people who want to preserve their ability to discriminate."[23]

A Time for Decision

Here is how Edward Gibbon, in his monumental six-volume classic work, *The Decline and Fall of the Roman Empire*, described the Goths' sack of Rome in AD 410:

In the hour of savage license, when every passion was inflamed, and every [moral] restraint was removed . . . a cruel slaughter was made of the Romans; and . . . the streets of the city were filled with dead bodies. . . . Whenever the Barbarians were provoked by opposition, they extended the promiscuous massacre to the feeble, the innocent, and the helpless.[24]

British historian Niall Ferguson has drawn parallels between the collapse of the greatest power of the ancient world and contemporary Europe. Like Rome, he writes:

Europe has allowed its defenses to crumble. As its wealth has grown, so its military prowess has shrunk, along with its self-belief. It has grown decadent in its malls and stadiums. At the same time, it has opened its gates to outsiders who have coveted its wealth without renouncing their ancestral faith.[25]

These words deserve a careful reading, as the same indictment could be applied to America where the sexual revolution rages, assaulting marriage and the natural family—with potentially disastrous consequences.

Just as the world of the early fifth century reacted with shock and horror at the sacking of "invincible" Rome, there is little to prevent a similar fate befalling a United States also crippled by moral decay. Such an unthinkable eventuality reminds us once again of the prophecy about the "merchants of the earth" who "weep and mourn" over the fall of the indomitable Mystery Babylon "because no one buys their cargoes anymore" (Revelation 18:11).

The real battle, however, is not political but spiritual—one that must be won one heart at a time. The darkness is always greatest before the dawn, and often it is when evil is at its height that the first rays of spiritual awakening appear. It is to the realm of the sacred that we now turn.

13

The Name That Overcomes

The time was June 1940—one year after Churchill's defiant speech to the British House of Commons—and the place was Dunkirk. The British Expeditionary Force, sent to stem the Nazi advance into Belgium and France, had been pushed steadily back to the sea.

A pall fell over England. Hitler's armies were poised to destroy the cornered Allied army. As the British people waited anxiously, a three-word message was transmitted from the besieged army trapped on the beaches at Dunkirk: *And if not*.

Would you or I know the meaning of that cryptic message? The British people recognized instantly both the origin of the communication and what it signified. *And if not* is found in the book of Daniel, where Shadrach, Meshach and Abednego defied Nebuchadnezzar, putting their trust in God. Their army was announcing to their compatriots across the English Channel: "Even if we are not rescued from Hitler's army, we will stand strong and unbowed."

The message galvanized the British people. Thousands of boats—everything from fishing trawlers to holiday sailboats—set out across the Channel in a gallant bid to rescue the Expeditionary Force. And they succeeded. Nearly 350,000 British and Allied soldiers were saved from the advancing Germans.

It was a different day, when the Church of England was a hallowed institution and English boys and girls were steeped in biblical stories from an early age. The British people were so conversant in Christian culture and understanding that they grasped immediately the meaning of an obscure biblical allusion regarding the noble intentions of their brave, trapped soldiers.

Metropolitan Hilarion's Exhortation

As Europe enjoyed an era of peace and growing prosperity after World War II, the inspiring testimonies of faith on the field of battle gradually faded from the collective memory, replaced by new generations for whom the horrors of war were only a history lesson. Materialism overcame matters of the spirit, and in country after country church attendance plummeted to single digits. It is perhaps no coincidence that those European countries that are facing a political crisis caused by the flood of refugees have long been experiencing a crisis of faith. According to a Eurobarometer Poll, 27 percent of those polled in Germany, 30 percent in the Netherlands, 34 percent in Sweden and 40 percent in France agreed with the statement "I don't believe there is any sort of spirit, God, or life force."[1]

Metropolitan Hilarion Alfeyev, a bishop of the Russian Orthodox Church and head of the Moscow Patriarchate's Department for External Church Relations, addressed the Synod on the Family convened by Pope Francis in October 2015. Metropolitan Hilarion called on the Catholic Church to counter challenges facing traditional marriage. While directed primarily to the

Christians of Europe, people of faith in the United States would also do well to heed his admonition. He pulled no punches in identifying what he believed to be the primary opponents of Christianity:

> I would like to use this opportunity to call my brothers in the Catholic Church to create a common front in order to defend Christianity in all those countries where it is being marginalized or persecuted. In Europe and America we witness growing pressure from those representatives of militant secularism and atheism who attempt to expel Christianity from the public square, to ban Christian symbols, to destroy traditional Christian understanding of the family, of marriage as a union between a man and a woman, of the value of human life from conception till natural death.[2]

Metropolitan Hilarion also addressed the growing number of Protestant communities that "preach moral ideals incompatible with Christianity." He criticized churches that bless same-sex unions or call for the "replacement of crosses from the church with the Muslim crescent. . . . We are witnessing the betrayal of Christianity by those who are prepared to accommodate themselves to a secular, godless, and churchless world."[3]

There would be much reason for discouragement were it not for the promise of Jesus regarding His Church: "The gates of Hades will not overcome it" (Matthew 16:18). Recalling the possible connections between the "gateway to Hades" in ancient Hierapolis and Gog and Magog, there is reason for hope that the seemingly unstoppable assault upon the Church in Europe and the United States will in the end fail.

The 21st Martyr

In an age of tremendous fear and uncertainty, Jesus encourages His disciples: "Take heart! I have overcome the world" (John

181

16:33). The world is witnessing spiritual revival as well as a powerful and unprecedented outpouring of the miraculous. Reports are multiplying of those who have little or no knowledge of Christianity coming to faith, including those living in the lands of Gog and Magog.

In February 2015 ISIS released a horrific video showing a group of men wearing orange jumpsuits being executed on a beach in Libya. The victims were identified as 21 Coptic Christian laborers. The scrolling caption announced their crime as being "people of the cross, followers of the hostile Egyptian Church."[4] The men had traveled to Libya in search of work before they were kidnapped, marched onto the beach and executed by knife-wielding Islamists. To a man they refused to renounce their faith, each dying with the invocation "Lord Jesus Christ" on his lips.

The self-identification of the murderers as members of the "Tripoli Province" of ISIS highlighted the appeal of the Islamic State. Unlike al-Qaeda, which does not view holding territory as its primary goal, ISIS is, as we have seen, committed to restoring a transnational Muslim state governed by sharia law.

The organization took root in Libya and the resultant Arab Spring, which swept across North Africa and the Middle East in 2011–2012, was applauded and supported by many in the West who naïvely believed it would bring democracy to the region. In reality the movement unleashed a wave of violence and chaos whose effects are being felt in Europe as waves of refugees and migrants arrive, with no end in sight. Those left behind have suffered terribly, especially Christians and other minorities targeted as infidels.

News reports of the killings on the beach in Libya mentioned "21 Copts." The Egyptian government, however, could confirm only twenty victims, leading to the mystery of the 21st hostage. It would later be revealed that he was a citizen of the

African country of Chad who had befriended the Copts and was captured along with them. The young man witnessed the incredible bravery of his friends in the face of imminent death.

Finally his turn came, and the young man's interrogator demanded that he embrace Islam. Though not a Christian, he was so moved by the faith of his companions that when asked, "Do you reject Christ?," he replied: "Their God is my God." He was summarily beheaded along with his newfound brothers.[5]

After witnessing the persecution of Christians, the early Church father Tertullian noted famously that "the blood of the martyrs is the seed of the Church." We may only in heaven learn about all the lives that were changed as news of the Christians beheaded for their faith on the beach in Libya was broadcast around the world.

Reports are multiplying by the hundreds and thousands of those who have experienced miraculous conversion. According to a report in *Mission Network News*, Christian aid organizations had been providing aid to the refugees in a United Nations camp that was under the control of Islamists. An ISIS fighter in northern Syria went to visit his relatives in one such camp that had several fundamentalist Muslim mosques and was a hotbed of radicalism.

The young man became enraged when he learned the source of the assistance they had been receiving. Considering it a humiliation for Muslims to receive help from infidels, he determined to find and kill the Christian workers. After witnessing the love of the Christians, however, he realized that he had been brainwashed. The Christians were nothing like the devils they were portrayed as being by the Islamists. He responded to the Gospel and became a Christian.

"He first saw how Islam brainwashed him about Christianity, and how that contrasted with the reality of what he saw in the Christians," the ministry director said. The young man was so enthusiastic about his new faith that he was placing himself in jeopardy: "He even got threats from [extremists], and that's when I began trying to calm him down, because otherwise they may kill him."[6]

Heaven's Secret Weapon

Churchill, in his monumental *The Second World War*, tells the story of a European envoy sent to discuss war preparations with Soviet leader Joseph Stalin. When the diplomat suggested that Stalin take steps to ease the plight of Catholics in Russia in order to improve relations with the Vatican, the atheistic dictator scoffed: "The Pope? How many divisions does he have?" Stalin, an ex-seminarian, left the Orthodox church in his youth after becoming convinced that belief in God was meaningless superstition that must be suppressed. During his rule tens of thousands of churches were closed and the faithful suffered mass arrests, with millions suffering martyrdom.[7]

Faith and religion, however, would have the last word. Fast-forward to the height of the Cold War in 1981. Tensions were high between the Soviet Union and the West, which was led by vigorous anti-Communists Ronald Reagan and British Prime Minister Margaret Thatcher. Determined to maintain its grip on Eastern Europe, the Soviet Union was threatening to intervene militarily in Poland to suppress the pro-democracy movement Solidarity—just as it had invaded Czechoslovakia in 1968 and Hungary in 1956.

But this time, things would turn out differently. Pope John Paul, who hailed from Poland, resolved that his homeland would not be overrun by the Soviets. Accordingly, he sent word to the Kremlin that if the Soviet Union invaded Poland, he would personally take his stand between the tanks and the Polish people.

Soviet leader Leonid Brezhnev wisely backed down. The battle of the wills between a man of faith and a great atheistic world power proved to be the turning point in the Cold War. In the years following, Poland made the transition to democracy, and within a decade the Soviet Empire would cease to exist.

God is not impressed with military might but rather blesses those who seek His face: "His pleasure is not in the strength of the horse, nor his delight in the legs of the warrior; the LORD delights in those who fear him, who put their hope in his unfailing love" (Psalm 147:10–11).

The Lord seeks those who will follow Him wholeheartedly. One such person can be sufficient to deflect God's judgment: "I looked for someone among them who would build up the wall and stand before me in the gap on behalf of the land so I would not have to destroy it, but I found no one" (Ezekiel 22:30).

Truly it was such as those whose stories we read on these pages that the prophet of old spoke of when he declared that "the people living in darkness have seen a great light; on those living in the land of the shadow of death a light has dawned" (Matthew 4:16). That same Light stands ready to heal our hearts and our lands, and even to spare us from great evil to come, for we also read: "And they overcame him because of the blood of the Lamb and because of the word of their testimony" (Revelation 12:11 NASB).

While the Scriptures warn of judgment upon nations that disobey God's law, there is also a great hope of forgiveness and restoration: "If my people, who are called by my name, will humble themselves and pray and seek my face and turn from their wicked ways, then I will hear from heaven, and I will forgive their sin and will heal their land" (2 Chronicles 7:14).

It cannot be denied that the Scriptures speak of evil times to come: "For then there will be great distress, unequaled from the beginning of the world until now—and never to be equaled again" (Matthew 24:21). Nations the world over will doubtlessly experience horrors like those described on these pages. Yet there is reason for great optimism, for we are promised that through spiritual revival God will forgive our sin *and will heal our land*. We can experience miraculous healing and restoration both on a personal and a national level.

Above all, let the reader be encouraged by His wonderful promise: "And surely I am with you always, to the very end of the age" (Matthew 28:20).

Even so, come quickly, Lord Jesus!

Afterword

The Atomization of Biblical Prophecy

> For the time will come when people will not put
> up with sound doctrine. Instead, to suit their own
> desires, they will gather around them a great num-
> ber of teachers to say what their itching ears want
> to hear.
>
> 2 Timothy 4:3

September 2015 was trumpeted by prophecy teachers, books
and websites as the perfect storm of biblical eschatology: a one-
month period when an astonishing convergence of apocalyptic
signs would shake the earth to its very foundation. Students of
the end times eagerly awaited the consummation of mysterious supernatural events long awaited by Christians since the
first century.

While careful to deny that they were setting dates, many of
the September 2015 prophecy teachers and writers left little
doubt that they expected the imminent fulfillment of major prophetic events, as indicated by titles such as Mark S. Hoffmeister's

Fifteen Days in September That Will Change the World (CreateSpace, 2015) and T. W. Tramm's *2015—The Final Jubilee?* (Tramm, 2015).

In *The Mystery of the Shemitah*, author Jonathan Cahn argued that America is a second Israel and was being judged by the seven-year Sabbath law called "shemitah" that was given to ancient Israel. Cahn presented evidence that stock market collapses and other cataclysmic events could occur at the end of the upcoming seven-year cycle on September 13, 2015. Despite denying that he was setting dates, he nonetheless considered his book to contain disclosures for our time: "Much that will be revealed in this book has never before been revealed in written form."[1]

John Hagee popularized the idea that lunar eclipses have historically coincided with major events in Jewish history and that a tetrad—or series of four lunar eclipses in 2014 and 2015—would fulfill major biblical prophecies. The last of these "blood moons" was set to occur on September 27, 2015, a date that Hagee confidently predicted would trigger something momentous: "The coming four blood moons points to a world-shaking event that will happen between April 2014 and October 2015. . . . God is sending planet Earth a signal that something big is about to happen."[2]

Prophecy teachers pointed to other so-called portents surrounding September 2015, including the inauguration of a Jubilee year—the fiftieth of the Jewish calendar—on the thirteenth of the month. Both the Feast of Tabernacles and Yom Kippur also fell in September. Others warned that the completion of the Jade Helm U.S. domestic military exercises on September 15 would lead to martial law and Christians being herded into "re-education camps."[3]

In the months leading up to September a number of prophets foretold an asteroid strike in the Caribbean on September 24 that would cause the rotation of the earth to stop for three days. A "magnitude 12 earthquake" and subsequent tsunamis would devastate the East Coast of the United States, Mexico, central and southern America, causing millions of casualties.[4]

On the basis of the prophecy that he claimed was dictated to him by God, evangelist Efrain Rodriguez announced that the imminent asteroid strike would cause "750,000 plus casualties" in Puerto Rico and millions worldwide.[5]

Despite the growing anticipation—a Google search of "September 2015 prophecies" generates more than a million hits—prophecy enthusiasts would have to continue waiting as the month passed with little fanfare. While more than a few prophecy teachers denied that they meant to imply that September 2015 had any special significance,[6] many students of biblical eschatology were wondering, What went wrong?

Seal Up the Words of This Prophecy

The apostle Paul's foretelling of a day when those who reject "sound doctrine" are drawn to teachers who tell them "what their itching ears want to hear" (2 Timothy 4:3) is an apt description of those who misinterpret prophecy and their followers. The so-called experts in the area of prophecy often find themselves under pressure to come up with the "next big idea" that will keep their followers entertained—and generate sales for their next book.

Instead of viewing minor divergences in the prophetic passages as complementary—i.e., describing the same events from the perspective of another biblical writer—prophecy teachers began to teach that the differences indicated completely separate events.

These novel additions are often based as much upon today's news headlines as they are upon the Bible. The prophetic timetable is steadily enlarged and expanded to take into account the "discovery" of all these additional events, resulting in prophecy charts showing highly detailed timelines of eschatological events. To please the "itching ears" of their followers, prophecy teachers feel constrained to show how their prophetic timelines fit with contemporary events—and to suggest specific dates when these events might take place.

By so doing such teachers come perilously close to committing the error of setting the date of prophetic events, which was specifically warned against by Jesus: "But about that day or hour no one knows, not even the angels in heaven, nor the Son, but only the Father" (Matthew 24:36).

Unfortunately, we are witnessing a growing number of prophecy teachers who insist that they are not dogmatically setting dates, but whose books are premised upon sensational revelations about the imminent fulfillment of prophetic events. By doing so they ignore the divine instruction given to Daniel at the conclusion of his visions of the future: "But you, Daniel, roll up and seal the words of the scroll until the time of the end" (Daniel 12:4). There is a mystical component that is inherent in the apocalyptic texts, which employ enigmatic symbolism that defies unambiguous categorization.

Thus all neatly laid out blueprints for the prophetic future have their shortcomings. A major drawback of the whole enterprise is the "atomization" of biblical prophecy. The dictionary defines *atomize* as (1) to reduce to minute separate units or (2) to subject to atomic bombing. While it may be true that either of these definitions at times rightly describes what expositors do to the biblical text, we will address the first. That is, not content to address the general prophetic themes that have been held by Christians throughout history, teachers compete with each other in "breaking apart" prophetic passages into smaller and smaller distinct units.

190

Signs of the Prophetic Future

The fundamental beliefs about the prophetic future that have always been held by the majority of Christians are set forth by Jesus in the Olivet Discourse (see Matthew 24, Mark 13, Luke 21). Jesus paints a grim picture of the future when His disciples ask: "What will be the sign of your coming and of the end of the age?" (Matthew 24:3).

A Great Rebellion

First, despite our best efforts to suppress evil and improve the lot of mankind, one day there will be a final great rebellion against heaven marked by a vicious assault upon the disciples of Jesus:

> Jesus answered: "Watch out that no one deceives you. For many will come in my name, claiming, 'I am the Messiah,' and will deceive many. You will hear of wars and rumors of wars, but see to it that you are not alarmed. Such things must happen, but the end is still to come. . . . All these are the beginning of birth pains.
>
> "Then you will be handed over to be persecuted and put to death, and you will be hated by all nations because of me. At that time many will turn away from the faith and will betray and hate each other, and many false prophets will appear and deceive many people. Because of the increase of wickedness, the love of most will grow cold, but the one who stands firm to the end will be saved."
>
> Matthew 24:4–6, 8–13

The Great Tribulation

Second, at the end of the age the world will descend into a dark period of human history marked by unprecedented horrors and suffering:

191

"For then there will be great distress, unequaled from the beginning of the world until now—and never to be equaled again. If those days had not been cut short, no one would survive, but for the sake of the elect those days will be shortened. At that time if anyone says to you, 'Look, here is the Messiah!' or, 'There he is!' do not believe it. For false messiahs and false prophets will appear and perform great signs and wonders to deceive, if possible, even the elect."

Matthew 24:21–24

The Last Battle

Third, this "reign of wickedness" will lead to the ultimate confrontation between God and the forces of evil, a battle that will be accompanied by terrible signs in the heavens and culminate in the Second Coming of Jesus Christ:

"Immediately after the distress of those days 'the sun will be darkened, and the moon will not give its light; the stars will fall from the sky, and the heavenly bodies will be shaken.' Then will appear the sign of the Son of Man in heaven. And then all the peoples of the earth will mourn when they see the Son of Man coming on the clouds of heaven, with power and great glory. And he will send his angels with a loud trumpet call, and they will gather his elect from the four winds, from one end of the heavens to the other."

Matthew 24:29–31

The Day of Judgment

Fourth, the final confrontation will be followed by a day of reckoning for all humankind, alluded to by Jesus in His contrasting of the good and the evil servant. The faithful servant will be rewarded, but the wicked servant will receive punishments for his actions:

"Who then is the faithful and wise servant, whom the master has put in charge of the servants in his household to give them their food at the proper time? It will be good for that servant whose master finds him doing so when he returns. Truly I tell you, he will put him in charge of all his possessions. But suppose that servant is wicked and says to himself, 'My master is staying away a long time,' and he then begins to beat his fellow servants and to eat and drink with drunkards. The master of that servant will come on a day when he does not expect him and at an hour he is not aware of. He will cut him to pieces and assign him a place with the hypocrites, where there will be weeping and gnashing of teeth."

Matthew 24:45–51

While much fruitful discussion is surely to be had in exploring the other eschatological passages, it is important to keep in mind that the above concise timetable of eschatological events is the specific answer given by Jesus to His disciples' question about end time events. To go further is to tread on less certain and more controversial territory. To be sure, some will want to expand this brief presentation to include other detailed events. Those who do so might consider the aphorism "Let us speak loudly where the Bible speaks loudly, and softly where the Bible speaks softly."

How Many Final Battles?

The Western mind places great emphasis upon the rational faculties. Science has no place for mystery, and we are uncomfortable with anything that cannot be reduced to clear delineation. God's purposes, however, are infinitely beyond human comprehension, and there will always be an element of mystery to our faith: "'For my thoughts are not your thoughts, neither are your ways my ways,' declares the LORD. 'As the heavens are higher than the earth, so are my ways higher than your ways and my thoughts than your thoughts'" (Isaiah 55:8–9).

Apocalyptic literature, which employs imagery and symbolism to convey truths about the future, especially reflects the element of mystery. The very nature of this literary genre defies mathematical precision. That is why various well-meaning attempts to chart precisely the prophetic future invariably contradict each other, as Paul Thigpen observed:

> The resulting discussions throughout conservative, evangelical and charismatic/Pentecostal circles are uncovering a bewildering array of conflicting teachings. Supporters of each position claim a biblical basis for their thought, and point to respected Christians of the past whose thinking apparently agrees with them.[7]

The reader will quickly detect that the present offering eschews the typical approach, which attempts to provide an unambiguous answer to every question about biblical prophecy. Rather, on these pages one will find a healthy respect for the element of mystery that is essential to the eschatological texts—and for the various outcomes that might be possible within the breadth of the sovereignty of God.

The battle of Gog and Magog is a prime example of the atomization of biblical prophecy. Admittedly, the account of that great end time battle in Ezekiel 38 and 39 differs in some respects from the battle of Gog and Magog described in Revelation 20, in no small part due to the fact that in the latter passage only four scant verses are devoted to the battle.

The atomizing solution is to separate the accounts in Ezekiel and Revelation to create two completely different battles. Those holding to the Russian invasion theory further separate Gog and Magog from the battle of Armageddon. This despite the incongruous situation of Russia and its confederates supposedly being annihilated in the battle of Armageddon a short time after already being completely destroyed in the war of Gog and Magog.

A considerable portion of the text in Ezekiel 38 and 39 is given to a vivid description of the final, utter destruction of Gog and company at the hand of the Lord. But perhaps most telling is the proclamation of the Lord after their defeat: "I will make known my holy name among my people Israel. I will no longer let my holy name be profaned, and the nations will know that I the LORD am the Holy One in Israel" (Ezekiel 39:7).

This creates more problems for those who hold to the theory of two battles. The book of Revelation says that the beast will open his mouth "to blaspheme God, and to slander his name and his dwelling place and those who live in heaven" (Revelation 13:6). Likewise, Paul describes the profanity of the "man of lawlessness" who "will oppose and will exalt himself over everything that is called God or is worshiped, so that he sets himself up in God's temple, proclaiming himself to be God" (2 Thessalonians 2:3–4).

The question is, When does this blasphemy take place? The commonly accepted view puts it after the battle of Gog and Magog in the time leading up to the final battle of Armageddon. But this cannot be, for after the battle of Gog and Magog the world will no longer be filled with blasphemy against the true God.

Scripture has a name for this final confrontation in which the Lord defeats the forces of evil. It is generally referred to as "the Day of the Lord," spoken of by the prophet Joel:

> "The sun will be turned to darkness and the moon to blood before the coming of the great and dreadful day of the LORD. And everyone who calls on the name of the LORD will be saved; for on Mount Zion and in Jerusalem there will be deliverance, as the LORD has said, even among the survivors whom the LORD calls. In those days and at that time, when I restore the fortunes

of Judah and Jerusalem, I will gather all nations and bring them down to the Valley of Jehoshaphat. There I will put them on trial for what they did to my inheritance, my people Israel, because they scattered my people among the nations and divided up my land."

Joel 2:31–3:2

On balance, the scriptural evidence indicates that this apocalyptic Day of the Lord is the final day of human history when the Lord intervenes to put an end to all evil rebellion. It is Gog and Magog, the Antichrist and Armageddon all rolled into one climactic struggle. In the announcement of the battle of Gog and Magog, Ezekiel confirms: "It is coming! It will surely take place, declares the Sovereign LORD. This is the day I have spoken of" (Ezekiel 39:8).

Notes

Chapter 1: Out of the Far North

1. John F. Walvoord, *Armageddon, Oil, and the Middle East,* rev. ed. (Grand Rapids: Zondervan, 1990), 141. See also Herman A. Hoyt, *The End Times* (Chicago: Moody, 1969), 152, and many others.

2. Mark Twain, *The Innocents Abroad* (San Francisco: American Publishing, 1869), https://www.gutenberg.org/files/3176/3176-h/3176-h.htm.

3. Ibid.

4. Compare the *New American Standard Bible*, which reads, "They are living securely, all of them" (Ezekiel 38:8).

5. Mark Hitchcock, *After the Empire: Bible Prophecy in Light of the Fall of the Soviet Union* (Wheaton, Ill.: Tyndale, 1994), 63.

6. The classic treatment of the topic remains W. F. Albright, "Gog and Magog," *Journal of Biblical Literature* 53 (1924): 378–385. See also J. I. Meyers, "Gog and the Danger from the North in Ezekiel," *Palestine Exploration Fund Quarterly* 64 (1932): 213–219.

7. Flavius Josephus, *Antiquities of the Jews* 1, vi, 1, as cited by Edwin M. Yamauchi, *Foes from the Northern Frontier: Invading Hordes from the Russian Steppes* (Eugene, Ore.: Wipf and Stock, 1982), 22.

8. Louis Bauman, *Russian Events in the Light of Biblical Prophecy* (Philadelphia: Balkiston, 1947), 23–25, cited in J. Dwight Pentecost, *Things to Come: A Study in Biblical Eschatology* (Grand Rapids: Zondervan, 1958), 328.

9. See "Rosh" in I. Howard Marshall, ed., *New Bible Dictionary* (Downers Grove, Ill.: InterVarsity, 1996), 423.

10. See "Meshech," ibid., 423.

11. Joseph Blenkinsopp, *Ezekiel* (Louisville: John Knox, 1990), 181.

12. *Antiquities of the Jews* 1, vi, 2.

13. Hal Lindsey and C. C. Carlson, *The Late Great Planet Earth* (Grand Rapids: Zondervan, 1970), 63.

14. Walter Eichrodt, *Ezekiel: A Commentary* (Philadelphia: Westminster Press, 1970), 518.

Chapter 2: Invasion from the East

1. Lindsey and Carlson, *The Late Great Planet Earth*, 86. See also Walvoord, *Armageddon, Oil, and the Middle East*, 179.

2. Carrie Gracie, "Xinjiang: Has China's crackdown on 'terrorism' worked?," *BBC*, January 2, 2015, http://www.bbc.com/news/world-asia-30373877.

3. Leith Fadel, "Chinese Military Advisors Expected to Join the Russians in Syria," *Al Masdar News*, September 27, 2015, http://www.almasdarnews.com /article/chinese-military-advisors-expected-to-join-the-russians-in-syria/.

Chapter 3: The Gates of Alexander

1. Josephus, *War of the Jews* 7, vii, 4, *Project Gutenberg*, January 10, 2009, http://www.gutenberg.org/files/2850/2850-h/2850-h.htm.

2. Cassandra Eason, *Fabulous Creatures, Mythical Monsters, and Animal Power Symbols: A Handbook* (Westport, Conn.: Greenwood, 2008), 29.

3. Noah Wiener, "Hierapolis and the Gateway to Hell," *Biblical Archaeology*, April 1, 2013, http://www.biblicalarchaeology.org/daily/biblical-sites-places /biblical-archaeology-sites/hierapolis-and-the-gateway-to-hell/.

Chapter 4: Battle of the Blood Drinkers

1. Mark Lallanilla, "Meet Vlad the Impaler, The Bloodthirsty Ruler Behind the Dracula Legend," *Huffington Post,* October 31, 2013, http://www.huffington post.com/2013/10/31/vlad-the-impaler-real-dracula_n_4181948.html.

2. Arnold Toynbee, *A Study of History* (Oxford: Oxford University Press, 1987), 116.

3. "The Battle of Vienna 1683," wien-vienna.com, undated, http://www.wien -vienna.com/vienna1683.php.

4. Leslie Benson records another instance of this bizarre practice in 1817, when "the hereditary Prince of Serbia . . . sent the stuffed head of (the usurper) Black George to Istanbul as a propitiating gift." See Leslie Benson, *Yugoslavia: A Concise History* (Chippenham, Wiltshire: Antony Rowe Ltd., 2001), 144.

5. John Bourne, "Total War I: The Great War," in *The Oxford Illustrated History of Modern War*, ed. Charles Townshend (Oxford: Oxford University Press, 1997), http://www.english.illinois.edu/maps/ww1/bourneessay .htm.

Chapter 5: The Muslim Savior

1. Byron Farwell, *Prisoners of the Mahdi* (New York & London: W.W. Norton & Company, 1989), 156–157.

2. Elizabeth Jackson, "Sounds of Summer: Gertrude Bell," *ABC News,* January 5, 2007, http://www.abc.net.au/pm/content/2006/s1821986.htm.

3. Shiryn Ghermezian, "Report: Jerusalem's Grand Mufti Planned Construction of 'Auschwitz-Like' Crematorium in Israel," *Algemeiner,* October 27, 2015, http://www.algemeiner.com/2015/10/27/report-jerusalems-grand-mufti -planned-construction-of-crematorium-in-israel/#.

4. "Yasir Arafat's Timeline of Terror," *CAMERA: Committee for Accuracy in Middle East Reporting in America,* November 13, 2004, http://www .camera.org/index.asp?x_article=795&x_context=7.

5. Cliff May, "Cutthroats of the Holy Land," *Townhall,* October 21, 2015, http://townhall.com/columnists/cliffmay/2015/10/21/cutthroats-of-the-holy -land-n2069011.

6. Lori Lowenthal Marcus, "The Muslim Brotherhood Is the Origin of All Islamic Extremism," *Jewish Press,* February 9, 2015, http://www.jewishpress.com /news/breaking-news/sisi-muslim-brotherhood-is-the-origin-of-all-islamic -extremism/2015/02/09/.

7. For my firsthand account of living near Bethlehem on the West Bank during those tumultuous years, see *The Gathering Storm* (Chosen, 1992).

Chapter 6: Holy War for the Promised Land

1. John Laffin, *Holy War: Islam Fights* (London: Grafton Books, 1988), 97.

2. "Omar, Covenant of," *Jewish Virtual Library,* 2008, http://www.jewish virtuallibrary.org/jsource/judaica/ejud_0002_0015_0_15095.html.

3. *Sahih Moslem,* English trans. (Beirut: Dar al Arabia, 1971), 4:1510.

4. Mark Banham, "Palestinian Children Taught 'How to Stab a Jew' Says Israeli UN Ambassador Danon," *International Business Times,* October 17, 2015, http://www.ibtimes.co.uk/palestinian-children-taught-how-stab-jew -says-israeli-un-ambassador-danon-1524470.

5. Ibid.

6. Raymond Ibrahim, "'Abducting Women' and 'Destroying Churches' is 'Real Islam'—Iraqi Ayatollah," *Human Events,* October 20, 2015, http:// humanevents.com/2015/10/20/abducting-women-and-destroying-churches -is-real-islam-iraqi-ayatollah/?utm_source=hedaily&utm_medium=email &utm_campaign=nl.

7. D. Shahid Abdul-Karim, "Ramadan Blessings," *Muslim Journal,* August 17, 2013, http://muslimjournal.net/ramadan-blessings-reflecting-on -the-progressive-leadership-in-the-community-of-imam-w-deen-moham med/.

8. Daniel Pipes, "The Danger Within: Militant Islam in America," *Commentary*, November 2001, http://www.danielpipes.org/77/the-danger-within -militant-islam-in-america.

9. Paul M. Barrett, *American Islam: The Struggle for the Soul of a Religion* (New York: Farrar, Straus and Giroux, 2007), 114.

10. Ibid., 115.

11. Paul M. Barrett, "One Imam Traces the Path of Islam in Black America," *Wall Street Journal*, October 24, 2003, http://www.wsj.com/articles/SB 106694267937278700.

12. Joshua Rhett Miller, "Controversial Imam to Join Jesse Jackson at Muslim Group's Banquet," *Fox News*, October 20, 2009, http://www.investigative project.org/1468/controversial-imam-to-join-jesse-jackson#.

13. Lord Carey, "Lord Carey: Britain Has a Duty to Rescue Syria's Christians," *Telegraph,* September 5, 2015, http://www.telegraph.co.uk/news/world news/middleeast/syria/11846651/Lord-Carey-Britain-has-a-duty-to-rescue -Syrias-Christians.html.

14. Scott Campbell, "Christians 'Martyred for Beliefs Every FIVE MINUTES by Islamic State and Other Terrorists,'" *Express*, September 20, 2015, http:// www.express.co.uk/news/world/606536/Christians-Islamic-State-martyred -Syria-religion-Assyrian-human-rights.

15. Lord Carey, "Lord Carey: Britain Has a Duty to Protect Syria's Christians."

Chapter 7: Camp of the Saints

1. Liz Sly, "As Tragedies Shock Europe, a Bigger Refugee Crisis Looms in the Middle East," *Washington Post,* August 29, 2015, https://www.washington post.com/world/middle_east/as-tragedies-shock-europe-a-bigger-refugee -crisis-looms-in-the-middle-east/2015/08/29/3858b284-9c15-11e4-86a3-1b5 6f64925f6_story.html.

2. Simon Kent, "Economist Warns: Germany's Migrant Invasion Will Lead to 'Massive Tax Increases,'" *Breitbart*, October 16, 2015, http://www.breitbart .com/london/2015/10/16/economist-warns-germanys-migrant-invasion-leaves -taxpayers-massive-tab/.

3. Daniel Greenfield, "The Death of Europe," *Accuracy in Media*, October 26, 2015, http://www.aim.org/guest-column/the-death-of-europe/.

4. Jerrold L. Sobel, "Islam and the Fall of Europe," *American Thinker*, October 20, 2015, http://www.americanthinker.com/articles/2015/10/islam_ and_the_fall_of_europe.html.

5. Jean Raspail, "The Fatherland Betrayed by The Republic," *GalliaWatch*, April 23, 2010, http://galliawatch.blogspot.com/2006/07/fatherland-betrayed -by-republic-by.html.

6. "Video: New 'Syrian' Immigrants in Europe Chant 'Allah give victory to Islam,'" *Conservative Papers,* September 9, 2015, http://conservativepapers .com/news/2015/09/09/video-new-syrian-immigrants-in-europe-chant-allah -give-victory-to-islam/.

7. Ann Corcoran, "Refugee Resettlement and the Hijra to America," *Washington D.C.: Center for Security Policy Press*, 2015, http://www.centerfor securitypolicy.org/wp-content/uploads/2015/04/Refugee_Resettlement _Hijra.pdf.

8. Daniel Greenfield, "The Syrian Refugee Crisis is Not Our Problem," *Frontpage,* September 4, 2015, http://www.frontpagemag.com/fpm/260020 /syrian-refugee-crisis-not-our-problem-daniel-greenfield.

9. Baron Bodissey, "A Nightmare Reborn," *Gates of Vienna,* September 17, 2015, http://gatesofvienna.net/2015/09/a-nightmare-reborn/.

10. Andrew G. Bostom, "Bat Ye'or: 'The Universal Caliphate Stands before Us,'" *American Thinker,* August 16, 2011, http://www.americanthinker .com/blog/2011/08/bat_yeor_the_universal_caliphate_stands_before_us .html.

11. Soeren Kern, "Germany's Muslim Demographic Revolution," *Gatestone Institute*, August 31, 2015, http://www.gatestoneinstitute.org/6423 /germany-muslim-demographic.

12. Ibid.

13. Corey Charlton, "ISIS Radicals Planning Terror Attacks in Europe ARE Entering the Continent Hidden among Migrants, Says German Police Chief," *Daily Mail,* November 26, 2015, http://www.dailymail.co.uk /news/article-3335489/ISIS-radicals-planning-terror-attacks-Europe-entering -continent-hidden-migrants-says-German-police-chief.html.

14. "Tausende Fluchtlinge Verlassen Unterkunfte aug eigene Faust," *Die Welt,* October 29, 2015, http://www.welt.de/politik/deutschland/article14 8206719/Tausende-Fluechtlinge-verlassen-Unterkuenfte-auf-eigene-Faust .html; quoted in Morris Schaffer, "Where oh Where Have the Muslim Migrants Gone?," *US Defense Watch,* November 3, 2015, http://usdefensewatch.com /2015/11/where-oh-where-have-the-muslim-migrants-gone/.

15. Ibid.

16. "Paris Attacks: Bataclan and Other Assaults Leave Many Dead," *BBC News,* November 14, 2015, http://www.bbc.com/news/world-europe-3481 4203.

17. "Holder of Syrian Passport Found in Paris Passed through Greece," *Reuters,* November 14, 2015, http://www.reuters.com/article/2015/11/14 /france-shooting-greece-idUSL8N13910Z20151114.

18. Graeme Wilson, "Young British Muslims 'Getting More Radical,'" *Telegraph,* January 29, 2007, http://www.telegraph.co.uk/news/uknews /1540895/Young-British-Muslims-getting-more-radical.html.

19. "ISIS Poses a Bigger Threat to U.S. Than Al Qaeda, FBI Chief Says," *ABC News,* July 23, 2015, http://www.nbcnews.com/storyline/isis-terror/isis-poses-bigger-threat-u-s-al-qaeda-fbi-chief-n396981.

20. "San Bernardino Shooting: Farook Tied to Jihadist Recruiter, Officials Say," *CNN Wire,* December 10, 2015, http://wnep.com/2015/12/10/san-bernardino-shooting-farook-tied-to-jihadist-recruiter-officials-say/.

21. Rick Noack, "Muslims Threaten Europe's Christian identity, Hungary's Leader Says," *Washington Post,* September 3, 2015, https://www.washingtonpost.com/news/worldviews/wp/2015/09/03/muslims-threaten-europes-christian-identity-hungarys-leader-says/.

22. Ibid.

23. "Nonwhite Invaders Riot on Hungarian Border after Le Pen Warns of 'Barbarian Invasion,'" *New Observer Online,* September 16, 2015, http://newobserveronline.com/nonwhite-invaders-riot-on-hungarian-border-after-le-pen-warns-of-barbarian-invasion/.

24. Sir Winston Churchill, *The River War* (London: Longmans, Green and Co., 1899), 2:248–250.

Chapter 8: Have You Come to Take Great Plunder?

1. Mariah Blake, "Let There Be Light Crude," *Mother Jones,* January-February, 2008, http://www.motherjones.com/politics/2008/01/let-there-be-light-crude.

2. Jonathan Cook, "Israel Stakes Claim to Golan after Oil Find," *Middle East Eye,* November 14, 2015, http://www.middleeasteye.net/news/israel-stakes-claim-golan-after-oil-find-913890970.

3. Tyler Crowe, "This Natural Gas Find Could Completely Change the World as We Know It," *The Fool,* November 3, 2013, http://www.fool.com/investing/general/2013/11/03/this-natural-gas-find-could-completely-change-the.aspx.

4. Hedy Cohen, "Eni's Egypt Gas Find Limits Israel's Export Options," *Globes: Israel's Business Arena,* January 9, 2015, http://www.globes.co.il/en/article-enis-egypt-gas-find-limits-israels-export-options-1001065749.

5. "Poll: Turkish People Dislike Israel Slightly More Than ISIS, Hezbollah, Hamas," *HaAretz,* November 3, 2014, http://www.haaretz.com/middle-east-news/1.624297.

Chapter 9: Beyond the Pillars of Hercules

1. Ptolemy, 28; *Geography,* l. 6. c. 7; cp. Pliny, *Natural History,* l. 6. c. 28.

2. "Bochart (in his 'Phaleg'), followed by many later scholars, identifies Tarshish with Tartessus, mentioned by Herodotus and Strabo as a district of southern Spain; he thinks, moreover, that 'Tartessus' is the Aramaic form

of 'Tarshish,'" in "Tarshish," Isidore Singer, ed., *Jewish Encyclopedia* (New York: Funk and Wagnalls, 1905), http://www.jewishencyclopedia.com/articles /14254-tarshish.

3. Herodotus, *The History*, i, 163, iv.

4. Dave Hunt, *A Woman Rides the Beast* (Eugene, Ore.: Harvest House, 1994), http://servantofmessiah.org/wp-content/uploads/downloads/2012/12 /A-Woman-Rides-the-Beast-by-Dave-Hunt.pdf.

5. Peter M. J. Stravinskas, ed., *Our Sunday Visitor's Catholic Encyclopedia* (Huntington, Ind.: Our Sunday Visitor, 1991), 175, 178.

6. Robert Broderick, ed., *The Catholic Encyclopedia* (Nashville: Thomas Nelson, 1976), 103–104.

7. R. W. Thompson, *The Papacy and the Civil Power* (New York: Harper and Brothers, 1876), 82.

8. Henry Kamen, *The Spanish Inquisition: A Historical Revision* (New Haven: Yale University Press, 1998), 253.

9. Edward Peters, *Inquisition* (Los Angeles: University of California Press, 1989), 87.

10. See "Constantinople" in Charles George Herbermann, *Catholic Encyclopedia* (New York: Robert Appleton, 1908), http://www.newadvent.org /cathen/04301a.htm.

Chapter 10: The One-Second War

1. "Electromagnetic Pulse: Effects on the U.S. Power Grid," *Federal Energy Regulatory Commission*, undated, http://www.ferc.gov/industries/electric /indus-act/reliability/cybersecurity/ferc_executive_summary.pdf.

2. R. James Woolsey and Peter Vincent Pry, "The Growing Threat from an EMP Attack," *Wall Street Journal*, August 12, 2014, http://www.wsj.com/articles /james-woolsey-and-peter-vincent-pry-the-growing-threat-from-an-emp -attack-1407885281.

3. James Woolsey and Peter V. Pry, "Op-Ed: Heading towards an EMP Catastrophe?," *Israel National News*, July 27, 2015, http://www.israelnationalnews .com/Articles/Article.aspx/17293#.VjVvBOx35ja.

4. Mark Langfan, "US Admits N. Korea, Maybe Iran, Can Now Target It with EMP-Nukes," *Israel National News*, April 12, 2015, http://www.israel nationalnews.com/News/News.aspx/193908#.Vjgw0ex35jY.

5. Woolsey and Pry, "The Growing Threat from an EMP Attack."

6. Jennifer Griffin, "Military Eyeing Former Cold War Mountain Bunker as 'Shield' against EMP Attack?," *Fox News*, May 5, 2015, http://www.fox news.com/politics/2015/05/05/military-eyeing-former-cold-war-mountain -bunker-as-shield-against-emp-attack/.

7. "National Space Weather Action Plan," *National Science and Technology Council,* October 2015, https://www.whitehouse.gov/sites/default /files/microsites/ostp/final_nationalspaceweatheractionplan_20151028.pdf.

8. Ibid.

9. Woolsey and Pry, "Op-Ed: Heading towards an EMP Catastrophe?"

10. Ibid.

11. Ibid.

12. Langfan, "US Admits N. Korea, Maybe Iran, Can Now Target It with EMP-Nukes."

13. Ibid.

14. Paul Bedard, "Expert: Iran Ships a Dry Run for Later Nuclear/EMP Attack; Humiliate Obama," *Washington Examiner,* February 14, 2014, http:// www.washingtonexaminer.com/expert-iran-ships-a-dry-run-for-later-nuclear emp-attack-humiliate-obama/article/2544041.

15. Woolsey and Pry, "Op-Ed: Heading towards an EMP Catastrophe?"

16. "Large Power Transformers and the U.S. Electric Grid," *U.S. Department of Energy,* June 2012, http://energy.gov/sites/prod/files/Large%20Power%20 Transformer%20Study%20-%20June%202012_0.pdf.

17. Woolsey and Pry, "Op-Ed: Heading towards an EMP Catastrophe?"

18. "Cybersecurity Incidents More Frequent and Costly, but Budgets Decline," *PWC Press Room,* September 30, 2014, http://press.pwc.com/News -releases/cybersecurity-incidents-more-frequent-and-costly-but-budgets -decline-says-pwc-cio-and-cso-global-sta/s/59769a8f-b9f7-43e1-8b54-2628b 18ef586.

19. Ted Koppel, *Lights Out: A Nation Unprepared, Surviving the Aftermath* (Danvers, Mass.: Crown, 2015).

20. "Ted Koppel Exposes Cyberattack Threat on U.S. Power Grid," *CBS News,* October 27, 2015, http://www.cbsnews.com/news/ted-koppel-exposes -cyberattack-threat-on-u-s-power-grid-in-lights-out/.

21. Steve Reilly, "Bracing for a Big Power Grid Attack: 'One is Too Many,'" *USA Today,* March 24, 2015, http://www.usatoday.com/story/news /2015/03/24/power-grid-physical-and-cyber-attacks-concern-security-experts /24892471/.

22. Griffin, "Military Eyeing Former Cold War Mountain Bunker as 'Shield' against EMP Attack?"

23. Woolsey and Pry, "Op-Ed: Heading towards an EMP Catastrophe?"

24. Ibid.

25. Nicole Homeier, et al, "Solar Storm Risk to the North American Electric Grid," *Lloyd's and the Atmospheric and Environmental Research,* 2013, http://www.lloyds.com/~/media/lloyds/reports/emerging%20risk%20 reports/solar%20storm%20risk%20to%20the%20north%20american%20 electric%20grid.pdf.

26. "Committee on the Societal and Economic Impacts of Severe Space Weather Events: A Workshop," *National Research Council of the National Academies*, 2008, http://www.nap.edu/read/12507/chapter/1.

27. Adam Mann, "1 in 8 Chance of Catastrophic Solar Megastorm by 2020," *Wired,* February 29, 2012, http://www.wired.com/2012/02/massive -solar-flare/.

28. Tony Phillips, "Near Miss: The Solar Superstorm of July 2012," *Science News*, July 23, 2014, http://science.nasa.gov/science-news/science-at -nasa/2014/23jul_superstorm/.

29. Maddie Stone, "What Would Happen If a Massive Solar Storm Hit the Earth," *Gizmodo*, August 20, 2015, http://gizmodo.com/what-would -happen-if-a-massive-solar-storm-hit-the-eart-1724650105.

Chapter 11: The Criminalization of Christianity

1. "Washington's Farewell Address 1796," *The Avalon Project—Yale Law School*, 2008, http://avalon.law.yale.edu/18th_century/washing.asp.

2. "Kim Davis, the Woman Behind Bars," *Liberty Counsel*, September 4, 2015, http://www.lc.org/newsroom/details/kim-davis-the-woman-behind -bars-1.

3. "Court of Appeals No. 14CA1351," Colorado Civil Rights Commission CR 2013–0008, August 13, 2015, https://www.courts.state.co.us/Courts/Court _of_Appeals/Opinion/2015/14CA1351-PD.pdf.

4. "Before the Commissioner of the Bureau of Labor and Industries of the State of Oregon," State of Oregon Bureau of Labor and Industries, Case Nos. 44–14 & 45–14, http://www.oregon.gov/boli/SiteAssets/pages/press /Sweet%20Cakes%20FO.pdf.

5. Barbara Boland, "Defiant Sweet Cakes Owners Have Until Monday to Pay Crushing $135k Fine," *Washington Examiner,* July 11, 2015.

6. Michael Paulson, "Can't Have Your Cake, Gays Are Told, and a Rights Battle Rises," *New York Times*, December 15, 2014, http://www.nytimes .com/2014/12/16/us/cant-have-your-cake-gays-are-told-and-a-rights-battle -rises.html?.

7. Jason L. Riley, "Atlanta Says It Terminated Its Fire Chief because He Published a Book Without Permission. The Real Reason is Because of What's in It," *Wall Street Journal,* November 10, 2015, http://www.wsj.com/articles /christian-belief-cost-kelvin-cochran-his-job-1447200885.

8. Ibid.

9. Ibid.

10. Ibid.

11. Jacob Tobia, "I am neither Mr, Mrs nor Ms but Mx," *Guardian,* August 31, 2015, http://www.theguardian.com/commentisfree/2015/aug/31/neither -mr-mrs-or-ms-but-mx.

12. "EEOC Sues Star Transport, Inc., for Religious Discrimination," Equal Employment Opportunity Commission Press Release, May 29, 2013, http://www .eeoc.gov/eeoc/newsroom/release/5-29-13.cfm.

13. Ibid.

Chapter 12: Darkest Before the Dawn

1. "U.S. Department of Education's Office for Civil Rights Announces Resolution of Civil Rights Investigation of California's Downey Unified School District," *United States Department of Education Office of Civil Rights*, October 14, 2014, http://www.ed.gov/news/press-releases/us-department-educations-office-civil-rights-announces-resolution-civil-rights-investigation-californias-downey-unified-school-district.

2. Ibid.

3. Tara Dodrill, "Lila Perry: Transgender Hillsboro High School Senior Sparks Walkout over Bathroom Use," *Inquisitr*, September 2, 2015, http://www.inquisitr.com/2387041/lila-perry-transgender-hillsboro-high-school-senior-sparks-walkout-over-bathroom-use/.

4. Michael E. Miller, "A transgender teen used the girls' locker room. Now her community is up in arms," *Washington Post*, September 2, 2015, http://www.washingtonpost.com/news/morning-mix/wp/2015/09/02/a-transgender-teen-used-the-girls-locker-room-now-her-community-is-up-in-arms/.

5. Emanuella Grinberg, "Controversy over Bathroom Access for Transgender Teen Divides Missouri Town," *CNN*, September 3, 2015, http://www.cnn.com/2015/09/03/living/missouri-transgender-teen-feat/#.

6. Ibid.

7. Dustin Higgins, "Obama Admin to Schools: Let Boys Use Girls' Bathrooms, or We Pull Funding," *Life Site News*, November 5, 2015, https://www.lifesitenews.com/news/obama-admin-to-schools-let-boys-use-girls-bathrooms-or-we-pull-funding.

8. Adelle M. Banks, "The Southern Baptist Convention has passed a resolution opposing gay marriage," *Washington Post*, June 17, 2015, https://www.washingtonpost.com/news/acts-of-faith/wp/2015/06/17/the-southern-baptist-convention-has-passed-a-resolution-opposing-gay-marriage/.

9. Ibid.

10. Ibid.

11. "Where Major Religions Stand on Same-Sex Marriage," *Pew Research Center*, July 2, 2015, http://www.pewresearch.org/fact-tank/2015/07/02/where-christian-churches-stand-on-gay-marriage/.

12. Ibid.

13. "Fast Facts about American Religion," *Hartford Institute for Religion Research*, undated, http://hirr.hartsem.edu/research/fastfacts/fast_facts.html#largest.

14. Ibid.

15. Joe Carter, "FactChecker: Are All Christian Denominations in Decline?" *Gospel Coalition*, March 17, 2015, http://www.thegospelcoalition.org/article/factchecker-are-all-christian-denominations-in-decline.

16. Mathew Block, "ELCA Has Lost Half a Million Members," *First Things*, June 4, 2013, http://www.firstthings.com/blogs/firstthoughts/2013/06/elca-has-lost-half-a-million-members.

17. Ibid.

18. Molly Hennessy-Fiske, "Houston Voters Reject LGBT Equal Rights Measure," *Los Angeles Times*, November 3, 2015, http://www.latimes.com/nation/nationnow/la-na-houston-nondisrcimination-vote-20151103-story.html.

19. David Walls, "City of Houston to Pastors: Turn over Your Sermons," *Texas Values*, October 14, 2014, https://txvalues.org/2014/10/15/city-of-houston-to-pastors-turn-over-your-sermons/.

20. Alexa Ura, "Houston Ordinance Vote is Test for LGBT Advocates," *Texas Tribune*, October 28, 2015, https://www.texastribune.org/2015/10/28/houston-ordinance-vote-next-big-test-lgbt-advocate/.

21. Jordan Rudner and Patrick Svitek, "A Simple Election Day, Mostly Yes or No Answers," *Texas Tribune,* November 3, 2015, http://www.texastribune.org/2015/11/03/election-day-some-races-more-charged-others/.

22. New York Times Editorial Board, "Support Houston's Equal Rights Ordinance," *New York Times,* November 2, 2015, http://www.nytimes.com/2015/11/03/opinion/support-houstons-equal-rights-ordinance.html?_r=0.

23. Hennessy-Fiske, "Houston Voters Reject LGBT Equal Rights Measure."

24. Edward Gibbon, *The Decline and Fall of the Roman Empire* (London: John Murray, 1846), 3:134.

25. Niall Ferguson, "Like the Roman Empire, Europe Has Let Its Defences Crumble," *Sunday Times*, November 15, 2015, http://www.thesundaytimes.co.uk/sto/comment/columns/NiallFerguson/article1633179.ece.

Chapter 13: The Name That Overcomes

1. "Biotechnology Report," *Directorate General Research, European Commission*, October 10, 2010, http://ec.europa.eu/public_opinion/archives/ebs/ebs_341_en.pdf.

2. Metropolitan Hilarion Alfeyev, "Metropolitan Hilarion's Speech to Synod of Bishops of the Catholic Church," *Bogoslov.Ru*, October 18, 2015, http://www.bogoslov.ru/en/text/2894022/index.html.

3. "Metropolitan Hilarion Calls on Catholics to Jointly Protect Traditional Marriage," *Interfax*, October 21, 2015, http://www.interfax-religion.com/?act=news&div=12422.

4. "ISIL video shows Christian Egyptians Beheaded in Libya," *Al Jazeera*, February 16, 2015, http://www.aljazeera.com/news/middleeast/2015/02/isil-video-execution-egyptian-christian-hostages-libya-150215193050277.html.

5. Fr. Thomas Philipose, "What Made a Non Believer Chadian Citizen Die for Christ Along with His '20 Coptic Christian Friends'?" Malankara Orthodox Syrian Church Diocese of Bombay, February 22, 2015, http://bombay orthodoxdiocese.org/what-made-a-non-believer-chadian-citizen-die-for -christ-along-with-his-20-coptic-christian-friends/.

6. Ruth Kramer, "Militants Bring Terror to Refugee Camps," *Mission Network News*, October 12, 2015, https://www.mnnonline.org/news/militants -bring-terror-to-refugee-camps/.

7. James M. Nelson writes: "Estimates of the total number all Christian martyrs in the former Soviet Union are about 12 million." See James M. Nelson, *Psychology, Religion, and Spirituality* (New York: Springer-Verlag, 2009), 427.

Afterword: The Atomization of Biblical Prophecy

1. Jonathan Cahn, *The Mystery of the Shemitah* (Lake Mary, Fla.: Charisma, 2014), 2.

2. "Four Blood Moons by John Hagee," *YouTube*, July 1, 2013, https:// www.youtube.com/watch?v=0kUf9kQdurQ#t=42. See also Todd Leopold, "Blood Moon Has Some Expecting End of the World," September 24, 2015, *CNN*, http://www.cnn.com/2015/09/01/living/blood-moon-biblical -prophecy-feat/. See also John Hagee, *Four Blood Moons: Something Is About to Change* (Franklin, Tenn.: Worthy, 2013). Similarly, Mark Blitz and Joseph Farah left little doubt that Bible prophecy would be fulfilled during the blood moons. See Mark Blitz and Joseph Farah, *Blood Moons: Decoding the Imminent Heavenly Signs* (Washington, D.C.: WND Books, 2014).

3. Mark Henricks, "US Military Exercise Sparks Fears of Martial Law," *Yahoo News* (July 18, 2015).

4. "The Truth About the September 2015 Asteroid Impact," *Astronotes*, June 29, 2015, http://www.armaghplanet.com/blog/the-truth-about-the -september-2015-asteroid-impact.html.

5. Jon Austin, "Reverend Whose 'Imminent' Asteroid Never Came Says Huge Space Rock Will STILL Hit Earth," *Express*, September 30, 2015, http://www.express.co.uk/news/science/608979/Reverand-whose-imminent -asteroid-never-came-says-huge-space-rock-will-STILL-hit-Earth. See also "Alert: Shocking News Cataclysm in Puerto Rico and the US Preparations— Efrain Rodriguez," YouTube, October 21, 2013, https://www.youtube.com /watch?v=CMGoPFjtcDg.

6. Others claimed that their predictions had actually come true. Jonathan Cahn, e.g., cited the overall poor performance of the stock market in 2015 as confirmation of his September 13 Shemitah prediction. See Troy Anderson,

"Jonathan Cahn Says Mystery of Shemitah Has Been Confirmed," *Charisma*, January 18, 2016, http://www.charismamag.com/spirit/prophecy/25370 -jonathan-cahn-says-mystery-of-shemitah-has-been-confirmed.

7. Paul Thigpen, "The Second Coming: How Many Views?," *Charisma & Christian Life*, February 1989, 42.

Index

Timothy J. Dailey has degrees from Moody Bible Institute (B.A. Bible, Theology), Wheaton College Graduate School (M.A. Theological Studies) and Marquette University (Ph.D. Religion and Ethics). He has also studied at Jerusalem University College and Hebrew University, Jerusalem.

Dr. Dailey has lived and taught on three continents. He met his Swiss wife, Rebekka, in Bethlehem, where their first two children were born. Dr. Dailey taught courses on theology and on the historical and archaeological background of the Bible at Bethlehem Bible College, the Jerusalem Center for Biblical Studies, and Biblical Resources Study Center. While living in Bethlehem during the Gulf War, Dr. Dailey wrote *The Gathering Storm* (Chosen, 1992)—the first of a dozen published books as well as numerous articles.

Since returning to the States, Dr. Dailey taught theology at Toccoa Falls College before becoming senior editor for Chuck Colson's nationally syndicated "BreakPoint" radio program. Dr. Dailey has also served as senior fellow for policy at the Family Research Council in Washington, D.C. He and Rebekka have five grown children and live in Northern Virginia.

Learn the Dark Truth behind Paranormal Phenomena

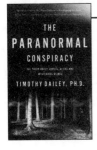

Teenage vampires. UFO sightings. Alien invasions. Ghost stories. The zombie apocalypse. Topics that once belonged to the fringes of the occult world are now on every television channel and magazine cover. So what does this mean for Christians? How do we respond to a culture saturated with the paranormal?

In this compelling book, Dr. Timothy Dailey confronts the counterfeit spirituality of the paranormal world head-on, exposing the dark truth behind these tales. Yet he offers hope: a way back to the one true source of spiritual connection. The only One that can satisfy our souls.

The Paranormal Conspiracy by Timothy Dailey, Ph.D.